Saying I Do was the Easy Part

0-8054-2430-X

Published by Broadman & Holman Publishers,
Nashville, Tennessee

Dewey Decimal Classification: 306
Subject Heading: MARRIAGE
Library of Congress Card Catalog Number: 00-068914

Unless otherwise indicated all Scripture quotations are taken from the Holy Bible, New Living Translation, © 1996, used by permission of Tyndale House Publishers, Inc., Wheaton, Ill., 60189, all rights reserved. Other Scriptures are marked AMP, The Amplified Bible, Old Testament © 1962, 1964 by Zondervan Publishing House, used by permission, and the New Testament © The Lockman Foundation 1954, 1958, 1987, used by permission; KJV, the King James Version; NASB, the New American Standard Bible, © the Lockman Foundation, 1960, 1962, 1963, 1968, 1971, 1972, 1973, 1975, 1977, used by permission; NIV, Holy Bible, New International Version, © 1973, 1978, 1984 by International Bible Society; and NKJV, New King James Version, © 1979, 1980, 1982, Thomas Nelson, Inc., Publishers.

Library of Congress Cataloging-in-Publication Data
Hlavka, Theda.
    Saying I do was the easy part : secrets to a dynamic and
fulfilling marriage
        p. cm.
    ISBN 0-8054-2430-X
    1. Marriage. 2. Marriage—Religious aspects—Christianity.
3. Wives—Conduct of life. 4. Wives—Religious life. I. Title.

HQ734.H67   2001
306.81—dc21
                                                            00-068914
                                                                  CIP

1 2 3 4 5 6 7 8 9 10 05 04 03 02 01

Foreword by Dennis Rainey

Saying I Do was the Easy Part

Secrets to a Dynamic & Fulfilling Marriage

THEDA HLAVKA

BROADMAN
&HOLMAN
PUBLISHERS

Nashville, Tennessee

To my three daughters, Joy, Heather, and Karen.
You are beautiful inside and out. I'm proud of each of you.
This book is for you.

To Alan, my husband, my very best earthly friend.
Thanks for your faithfulness to me.

To Jesus Christ, my everything.

CONTENTS

FOREWORD

For many who marry today, "I do" has been replaced with "I don't!" Sadly, those who are going for the "silver" and "gold" anniversaries are an endangered species. The "seven year itch" has now been cut in half by a divorce rate that soars its highest in the third and fourth year of marriage. And the marriage merger is viewed with such contempt by a new generation that more than 4 million have bypassed formal vows and opted for just living together.

Our nation's most basic unit, the family, is in trouble. Serious trouble.

In the midst of the confusion and despair, a remnant of clear, authoritative voices can be heard and need to be heard. Theda Hlavka is one of those voices. My wife Barbara and I really like Theda and her husband, Alan. We like hanging out with them. Laughing with them. They are real people. Real people you can relate to. Real people who have experienced life's gray moments found in the valleys and the magnificent views that come from the mountaintops. They have weathered the storms because they have anchored their union in the unchanging truth of Scripture and a secure commitment to Jesus Christ.

It is from the strength of this union that Theda shares timeless secrets that will give you the same advantages that they've enjoyed. With a gentle, yet firm hand, Theda shares practical biblical principles that will overhaul your mind and transform your marriage. *Saying I Do Was the Easy Part* is a quick read but a profound look at how your marriage was designed to transcend the rigors of everyday life and ultimately reflect the very character and nature of God.

Read this book. Live out its secrets in your marriage. You are in for a pleasant surprise as you sit at the feet of a gifted communicator and glean the wisdom of a faithful wife and mother.

By the end of this book, you're going to understand why Barbara and I really like Theda Hlavka. You will too.

DENNIS RAINEY
Executive Director
FamilyLife

ACKNOWLEDGMENTS

$\mathcal{T}$hanks to the friends who gave their time and energy to help me with this book. There were some who prayed, some who allowed me to use their stories (some names I've changed and others I haven't), and, of course, there were some who read the chapters as they came "hot off the presses" to give me their feedback: Deanne Bergh, Carole Buzza, Amy Campbell, Marian Castillo, Jody Dawes, Denny Deveny, Judy Drais, Tamera Hodges, Mindy Nelson, Kathy Norquist, Kim Peil, Ruth Schliecker, Jamie Van Zanten, Chris Welling, and Victoria Wolsborn. I'm genuinely grateful to each and every one of you. I love you.

I'm also deeply thankful to my friend Steve Tucker for his excellent editing and his always positive feedback. This book would still be in never-never land if it weren't for you. Thanks, friend.

Dale Allen, you and I both know this project would never have happened if it weren't for your sweet, persistent pushing. You are the nicest pushy person I've ever met. Thanks for the encouragement and the hours and hours you and Joyce have spent in prayer to see this book to completion.

For my husband, I can't say enough. He has been there for me through all the ups and downs. Alan, you have been my rock and ever-faithful friend. You are truly the best friend I've ever had on earth. Can you believe with our backgrounds that we actually have one of those rare and precious marriages? It's a modern-day miracle!

Without the Lord in my life, I would be spending eternity away from his presence right now. I can't imagine life without you, Lord. You make sense of everything. I owe you everything.

INTRODUCTION

*I*magine yourself standing on a ledge with thousands of other people. To your left is your boyfriend. To your right is a couple you've never seen before. Below you is a bottomless pit. In front of you, across a chasm, is another ledge.

As you watch, couples begin to jump, trying to reach the other ledge. They seem compelled to jump, as if they have no choice. You notice that most of them fall into the pit, some screaming, some crying, and others with a shocked expression on their faces, as if they can't believe they missed the ledge.

A few make it to the other side but just barely. They grab onto it with their hands, holding on for dear life, looking for some foothold that will allow them to climb onto the ledge.

Then you see a few who actually make it. *Yes*, you think, *it is possible.* Those who are on the other side are smiling, laughing, and hugging one another.

Soon you realize it's your turn. Your boyfriend grabs your hand. "C'mon, hon; let's give it a try," he encourages.

"I don't know," you reply. "I mean, look at all those people who aren't making it."

"We'll make it. I promise," he says.

"How do you know?" you ask.

"I just know," he says. "What's wrong with you anyway? I thought you loved me."

"I do love you," you say.

"Then let's jump," he says as he grabs your hand. "C'mon. It'll be fun."

"How can landing at the bottom of the pit be fun?" you ask.

"First of all, we're not going to land at the bottom of the pit. And second of all—" he begins.

The couple next to you anxiously asks, "You guys gonna jump, or what?"

"Yes, we're gonna jump. Just give us a minute," your boyfriend replies.

"We haven't got all day, you know. What's the holdup?" the man asks.

"Well, my girlfriend here isn't sure she wants to jump."

"Hey, it's no big deal," he says. "This is my third try, and I'm sure we'll make it this time."

"How can you be so sure?" you ask.

"Each time I learn something new. I found a great girl this time. I'm sure we'll make it," he says, grabbing the young woman's hand next to him. "She even looks like a jumper, doesn't she?"

You look at the young woman. You must admit she looks young and healthy. "What happens at the bottom of the pit?" you ask.

"Oh, you get a few bumps and bruises, but no big deal. Once your bones heal, and if you work hard enough, you can climb back up and start all over again," he replies. "But you have to be smart like me and find the right person. The first two I chose were real losers, but this time—"

"Hey, you guys gonna gab all day, or you gonna jump?" the next couple in line asks.

"I guess we're gonna jump," you say. "Right, hon?"

"Right!" your friend replies.

The funny thing about this scenario is that it happens many times each day. People get married thinking they're going to be the exception—they're the ones who will make it across the chasm to a happy, fulfilling marriage.

When you hear that 50 percent of all marriages end in divorce, it should make you take a second look. Of the 50 percent who stay married, only about 20 percent actually enjoy their marriages. The rest are hanging on by their fingernails. They're married, but they're not necessarily enjoying it.

If you asked people to jump a chasm, letting them know that their chances of actually making it were two out of ten, most people wouldn't jump. Why not? The odds aren't good. No one wants to take that kind of risk. Yet that's what thousands of couples do every month.

All couples that marry are looking for happiness and fulfillment, but many of them are headed for heartbreak and loneliness.

God intended marriage to be an exciting, dynamic, and fulfilling relationship. Next to our friendship with him, marriage should be the most complete and fulfilling friendship we have.

So, what's the secret? There are several. That's what this book is about—the secrets to having a dynamic and fulfilling marriage. By trial and error I've learned some of them over the nearly thirty years I've been married. Others I've learned by observing people—those with good marriages and those with bad ones. I've also learned them by studying God's love letter to me, the Bible.

If God created marriage, then he probably has some helpful things to say about how to make it work. When you buy a new appliance or gadget, it's always best to read the owner's manual first before you try to assemble or use it. The Bible is our owner's manual for marriage. The difficulty is that we often leave it on the shelf and wonder why our lives are so messed up.

RUTH AND JIM

At first Ruth and Jim forgot to follow God's manual.

At eighteen, Ruth was a typical impulsive and idealistic young woman. The first time she saw Jim walking across campus, she knew he was for her. "That's the man I'm going to marry," she told her friend. She and Jim began dating and seven months later stood on the ledge of marriage and jumped.

"I entered marriage looking for what I could get out of it. I wanted Jim to meet my needs," Ruth confesses. She realized right away that the open, talkative man she knew before they got married was really very quiet and withdrawn. His fears and insecurities showed up more and more as the marriage progressed.

Thirty years and three children later, the marriage finally unraveled. It had been unraveling bit by bit over time, but when Jim confessed to a three-year affair, Ruth was devastated. Suicide seemed a reasonable solution.

A friend gave Ruth a book about prayer, and she began to read it. "The book talked about telling God how much you love him," Ruth said, "so I began to do that. At first it was just words, but then it became more and more real. For the first time in my life, I realized I was a person of worth—not because of anything I'd done, but because God loved me. His love was totally unconditional! It was a radical concept, which led me to make some drastic changes in my life."

"I purposed in my heart to love Jim the way I was experiencing God's love for me," she continued. "I began doing things for him out of this love. I had no motive but to love Jim unconditionally. I was expecting nothing. I didn't even know if he would stay. Over the next nine months, I saw God love Jim through me. I was sort of a bystander, and I watched as God drew him [Jim] into his arms of love too."

Because of God's love through Ruth, Jim asked her forgiveness and went before the entire church to confess his sin.

"Everything was finally out in the open," Ruth confesses. "There was no more pretending. Together we began our life over."

Now, more than ten years later, Ruth says, "We are both very much aware that God has done an extraordinary work in the lives of two ordinary, broken people."

Ruth and Jim almost missed God's best for them. They were able to pick up the pieces, go back to the owner's manual, and start over. Today they counsel others on how to follow God's marriage manual.

You might as well know up front that unless you are committed 100 percent to following God's manual, your marriage won't work. You'll end up at the bottom of the pit with the rest of the ruined marriages, or at best, hanging onto the ledge. You can't pick and choose the principles you want to follow. It's all or nothing. There is no in-between. Either God knows everything about how a marriage should work or he knows nothing. If he knows everything, then it's in our best interest to learn and understand all he's said about marriage and the relationship between a man and a woman, and to follow it.

If you were having a problem with your computer, wouldn't it be incredibly helpful to have a personal visit from the person who thought it up and put it together? He or she would certainly know how to make it work properly. No doubt this person would be able to figure out what the problem was and to fix it.

Doesn't it make sense to go to the One who created marriage and to find out what he had in mind? His principles are simple but not easy and will require a lot of hard work. Most people want a great marriage, but they don't really want to do the work. After all, if having an awesome marriage were easy, everyone would have one.

I have a confession. I have a selfish reason for writing this book. I have three daughters. I want them to have the kind of marriage I've been privileged to enjoy. I want them to know the joy of an awesome marriage. I want them to experience the closeness of having their best friend with them throughout their lives. And I want them to avoid as many problems as possible in their future marriages.

I'm also thinking of some of my daughters' friends as I write these words. Many of them don't have positive role models—someone to show them how to keep from falling into the pit. They need someone to show them God's blueprint. They need to know that they, too, can have a strong, dynamic, loving, and wonderful marriage.

There are also many already-married women who have tried and can't seem to make this marriage thing work. They just don't know what to do. These principles are for them, too, whether they've been married a few days or many years. It's never too late to begin applying them.

It took Ruth and Jim thirty years before they really began reading and applying the principles from God's owner's manual. It took Alan and me ten years to fully understand what God wanted for our marriage. In the following pages, I will introduce you to Kathy, Ann, Carole, Amy, and many others, and share with you the lessons we have learned. Hopefully you can avoid some of the mistakes we made and benefit from the things we've done right, and by God's grace, you, too, can experience all God has for your marriage.

Chapter 1

A HUSBAND'S GREATEST SOURCE OF JOY

"Sit down, child," her father repeated for the fifth time. "You know he's not coming."

"Yes he is!" she said with more optimism than she felt.

She walked once again to the window to see if he might be coming. As she tiptoed to give herself every inch possible, she marveled at the colors in the sky. It was the perfect evening—the sky, with its multi-colored clouds dancing in the faint breeze; the trees, just reaching the peak of their kaleidoscope of autumn colors. Another sigh.

She felt her mother's gentle hand on her shoulder. "You must come sit down and eat something, dear. Stop torturing yourself like this."

She could feel the hot tears well up in her eyes as she looked at her mother. "He promised he would come."

"Men of his stature do not marry peasant women," her father's ever-rational, yet kind manner finally reaching through to her.

"Yes, I suppose I have been foolish to believe . . ." From the corner of her eye, she saw a faint glint on the horizon. Turning back to the window, she was once again on her tiptoes, straining with everything she had. Nothing. Had she only imagined it? Was the sun playing tricks on her eyes?

No! There it was again! And again! Her heart soared! Could it possibly be him? The one she dreamed of every night for a fortnight ever since their first meeting? He was everything she wanted and more. He was handsome and funny and charming and kind. On top of it all, he was a man of influence and very rich. She would have been happy if he'd been a man without fortune, but she wouldn't complain.

As she stared out the window, the distant figure began to take form. It was definitely a horse and rider, but was it *her* horse and rider? Who else would be coming at this time of night?

She stood on her tiptoes until her whole body ached. Then she realized that whoever it might be was close enough that she didn't have to tiptoe anymore. "Breathe," she told herself.

As the rider came even closer, she could see the color of his horse. It was white. "It must be him," she thought. At that moment she realized how terrible she looked. Even though she had put on her best dress and fixed her hair, the hours that had passed had taken its toll on both.

"Mother, hurry! I can't let him see me like this!" she screamed, panic setting in. The next few minutes were a whirlwind of flurry as mother and daughter ran around frantically, changing her clothes and fixing her hair.

"Father," she asked, "is it he?"

"I do believe it is, child. I do believe it is," he replied from his post at the window. She could tell he was smiling as he spoke. No one from their family had ever managed to marry someone so decidedly above their economic level. "He's here!"

She quickly ran to the chair designated for receiving guests and smoothed her dress. The rap on the door startled her and caused her pulse to quicken. "Breathe!" she told herself again.

"Welcome, sir!" she heard her mother saying.

As he came around the door, she stood. Their eyes met! Was that an explosion she heard? Perhaps her heart?

"I've come back just as I said!" his voice like the sound of a thousand cascading waterfalls.

A quiet yes was all she could manage.

Her eyes drank in the beauty of his whole being. There he was, her knight in shining armor. He looked so incredibly handsome in his uniform. She noticed he had taken off his helmet, and she could see his thick black hair and deep blue eyes. He even had a dimple when he smiled. She had forgotten how much she loved everything about him.

He was talking to her father! As she watched, her father began nodding his head vigorously with the biggest smile on his face she'd ever seen. Then, before she knew it, he walked to her side and knelt before her! She felt her head swim. He was going to ask her to marry him! *This must be a dream!* she thought. But no, it was real. She heard herself saying yes!

"Look at the size of that ring!" her mother whispered.

Then he took her head in his strong hands and kissed her ever so gently. His lips tasted like honey, and it took her breath away. As he bent to kiss her again, she heard a sound. What was it? She pushed it out of her brain so she could savor the moment. There it was again. It sounded like a baby crying. She tried pushing it out of her mind again, but it was no use. Why was the sound so familiar?

Jolted by the sound, she sat upright on her sofa. She'd fallen asleep again reading her romance novel. As she stumbled to the baby's room, she peeked in on her three-year-old son who had totally destroyed his room before he, too, had fallen asleep in the middle of the floor. She glanced at the clock. Her first and third graders would be home soon, and her husband would follow a few hours later. As she picked up her crying three-month-old infant, she got a whiff of a ripe diaper. "Don't breathe," she told herself. As she turned to lay her daughter on the changing table, she murmured, "Reality's the pits!"

Sound familiar? Unfortunately, reality often *is* the pits. The very things we were attracted to before we were married can become so aggravating that we want to scream. Why? Our perspective changes.

Think back to when you were first dating. What attracted you to your husband? I was first attracted to Alan by his good looks. I thought he was one of the best-looking guys on campus. As I got to know him, I discovered he was also easy to talk to. We discussed everything. We'd talk for hours. I was very attracted to this guy who was willing to share his innermost thoughts and was also genuinely interested in what I had to say.

Yet what attracted me thirty years ago could have become a source of conflict and irritation. *Why does he have to talk so much? Why does he have to tell me everything that goes on in his life? Why can't he just shut up?* You get the point.

Other wives have experienced similar scenarios. Instead of a husband who's a handsome jock, he's "obsessed with sports." A man who's ambitious becomes a "workaholic." A tender, compassionate mate becomes an "introspective boor." Do you see how we can take something positive and turn it into something negative? I think it's a much better use of our time to concentrate on the positive and rethink the negative. Ask yourself, "Why is it negative? Am I being overly picky? Is this really a positive that I've forgotten? Am I really the one who's changed?"

Think for a minute about a newborn. Do you nag him and try to get him to change his habits? Do you tell him not to cry in the middle of the night or make a mess in his diaper? Why not? Why don't you tell him to grow up and quit being such a baby?

We don't expect a baby to change. That precious bundle of joy has his negative habits, but we don't require him to change to fit our demands. So why do we do that to the man with whom we plan to spend the rest of our lives?

"Lydia" is a special woman. She's an incredible wife and mom. She's very industrious, planning her days so there's no wasted time. She's not afraid of hard work. She's creative, kindhearted, and also a working mom. She's the kind of woman you love to hate. How does she do it? She's obviously a unique woman. You can find her in Proverbs 31. Surprised?

Proverbs 31 has many insights into the role a wife is to play in the life of her husband. Lydia understood what it took to be a good wife.

At the same time, she was very strong and goal-oriented. As we look further into her life, it's obvious that her husband was a high priority for her. Let's see what we can learn from her.

"A wife of noble character who can find? She is worth far more than rubies" (v. 10 NIV). Her character is above reproach. She is priceless, difficult to replace. This woman is rare. Think for a minute about all the women you know. How do they stack up to these criteria? Sadly, not very well. I can only think of a handful of women who truly match up. You can see why she's so rare and valuable.

"Her husband has full confidence in her and lacks nothing of value" (v. 11 NIV). Take a second look at this verse. It is remarkable. "Her husband has *full* confidence in her. . . ." Another version is translated thus: "Her husband can trust her, and she will greatly enrich his life." He totally and completely trusts her. She must have convinced him over the years that she was trustworthy. Men are sometimes reluctant to share their innermost thoughts and feelings with us because they're not sure they can trust us with such guarded information. We must prove to them we're trustworthy and that they have nothing to fear. We must earn their trust.

I'd like to share part of a letter from a friend of mine whose wife was able to win his trust.

> Two or three years ago my wife's attitude toward me changed . . . . The change . . . toward me was such that I noticed it immediately, and it has never reverted since.
>
> When her attitude changed I was so encouraged, but I was afraid to mention it. I knew I hadn't done anything to earn it. And I guess I didn't expect it to last. I didn't want to break the bubble. After all, after that many years of marriage [more than twenty] I was trying to be thankful for the good aspects of our marriage and not expect much more. But I felt like I was permanently attached to a resident critic/doubter. But that's all history.
>
> You know what? Because she changed, I'm changing. I won't begin to identify with the model husband, but

having a receptive mate has made me want to be more appreciative, more expressive, more helpful, more considerate. I even want to open up to her more. Before, I was just handing her ammunition. But now I feel safe admitting shortcomings to her.

I thank God every day for the new wife I have. And every day I try to find ways to let her know how much I care for her. And I really love her more than I ever have.

Did you notice the part about how he now feels safe admitting his shortcomings? Before, he was just "handing her ammunition." It's crucial that we don't misuse the power we have in our marriages. It's not fair. Because we have a marriage license, we think we have the right to say whatever comes to our minds, which is often something negative. *We would never treat our friends the way we treat our husbands.*

Now let's take a look at verse 12: "She brings him good, not harm, all the days of her life" (NIV). This woman is in this thing for life. It's not just a year or two, but for "all the days of her life." She's careful about what she says and does. She measures her words and is careful to bring good and not harm to her man.

Recently Alan came to me and asked if he might have ten minutes of my time. I was in the middle of something (the story of my life), but I decided I could spare ten minutes. He began telling me about some things that were on his heart. I listened intently for the first few minutes. Soon ten minutes had come and gone with no signs of a conclusion, so I tried to concentrate on what he was saying but was having a difficult time. When twenty minutes came and went and no end in sight, I blurted out, "Is this going anywhere?" His reply: "Not anymore." I think Lydia would have frowned.

"She watches over the affairs of her household and does not eat the bread of idleness" (v. 27 NIV). We need to be careful not to get sucked into the modern-day "bread of idleness," that is, romance novels, soap operas, love stories, and so forth. They warp our thinking and make us unhappy with what we have. Real life isn't anything like the fantasies we watch and read. We can't maintain the level of emotion they portray—no one can. They make great stories, but they *do not* reflect reality. Besides, real life can be much more exciting and wonderful and fulfilling.

Now, look at what this woman's husband said. "Many women do noble things, but you surpass them all" (v. 29 NIV). Whoa! Not only did he notice positive things about the wives of other men, but he measured his wife against them and ranked her head and shoulders above the rest! For some reason, that appeals to me. It probably shouldn't, but it does. There's something satisfying about having your husband think you're the best thing around. It gives you the added incentive to keep on going. It makes you want to try even harder. It also gives you the security that your husband knows he won't find anything better "out there." Isn't that something worth working toward?

KATHY

Kathy has learned to be one of these women. Just ask Ron. When they met, it was love at first sight. She was seventeen. He was eighteen. Two years later they were married. "After only six months, I decided I'd married the wrong person, and the thought crossed my mind that maybe I should have my marriage annulled," says Kathy. The problem? She realized Ron wasn't perfect. So she spent the next twelve years trying to change him to fit into her neat little "husband" box.

According to Kathy, "We just have that inborn trait of wanting to fix, improve, change, and so forth. It never works, but we keep on trying! It's only when we quit and step out of the way that we can allow God to do his work." That's exactly what Kathy did. It was a gradual process, which involved several incidents that changed her perspective and thinking, and ultimately, her behavior.

One such incident occurred on a day when Ron was headed out to play golf—again. When Kathy quizzed him about why he was going to play golf instead of spending time with her, he said, "My buddies accept me just the way I am. They don't try to change me."

Another time, as she was poring over yet another "how-to" marriage manual, Ron walked by and said, "I wish you'd quit reading all those books and begin to apply them." Ouch!

At times Kathy was unhappy, and so was Ron. Something needed to change, and Kathy realized that she was the one. The old ways weren't working, and she hated the feeling of separation that sometimes came between them. She finally realized she couldn't control Ron, and he wasn't going to fit nicely into her "husband" box.

She worked at looking for ways to encourage him and build him up rather than focus on her own insecurities and need for him to "be a certain way." After six months Ron asked her what was going on and why everything was going so well. She shared with him the decision she'd made six months earlier.

The difference in their marriage was remarkable. Instead of being adversaries, they were becoming best friends. Slowly Kathy realized that the differences between them were good and not bad. She now sees how God uses Ron's strengths and weaknesses as catalysts to help her change and grow and become more Christlike. "I feel most fulfilled when Ron feels successful. I would rather see him succeed than see myself succeed."

I asked Ron how Kathy stood up against the Proverbs 31 woman after more than thirty years of marriage. He said, "On a scale of one to ten, Kathy is an eleven."

I'll conclude this chapter with a challenge. Recently I read the following article in an Ann Landers column.

> Several years ago, I tried [an] experiment with my husband. I had reached the point where I could barely tolerate being around him.
>
> I'm quite certain he felt the same about me because I never failed to tell him what I thought—and it was never complimentary. I considered divorce long and hard but knew I had really loved him once, and we did have children together. I decided a 30-day experiment was worth

the effort. For the next month, I did not utter a single negative word to my husband. I thought at times that I would explode from holding it in, but I survived. I repeated that experiment for a second month, and it was a little easier. I lost my temper only once. At the end of the third month, I actually was looking forward to my husband coming home from work. Six months after I began the experiment, our relationship had turned around completely. . . .

I would have missed out on the incredible life I now have with my husband if I hadn't tried that 30-day experiment.

Would you be willing to try this experiment? Is your marriage worth it? I realize this may be one of the most difficult things you'll ever do, but what have you got to lose except pride, selfishness, anger, and frustration? What have you got to gain? Everything! You might consider enlisting the help of one or two friends—a tongue-controlling accountability group. You owe it to your children, your husband, yourself, and most of all, your Lord. May your reality become more exciting, fulfilling, and enjoyable than any fantasy you could dream.

What kind of marriage would you have if you became your husband's loudest cheerleader? If his heart trusted in you? If you were his greatest source of joy on earth? That's something worth working for, isn't it?

Chapter 2

GET PAST YOUR PAST

She walked slowly but deliberately to the kitchen and carefully lifted her mother's butcher knife from the drawer. She could feel the weight of it. She ran her finger along the blade. It was sharp. She watched as her hands turned the blade toward her heart. She'd dreamed of this moment many times.

She dreamed of it when she felt the weight of caring for her five younger siblings—like last Saturday night, one of many, when her parents left with friends for a "night on the town." She couldn't sleep, worried they wouldn't return. She'd look outside every time she heard a car drive by, hoping that somehow it would be them. Slowly, the seconds and minutes would pass. Then, after what seemed an eternity, she'd see the headlights and know they were finally home.

She dreamed of it when she felt alone—sobbing in her room, hoping someone would hear, but fearful they'd discover she wasn't perfect.

She dreamed of it when everyone she knew was asked to the prom but her. She'd smile with her friends, pretending to be happy for them but wondering what was wrong with her.

She dreamed of it in the middle of the night when she'd awaken from yet another nightmare—one in which she was carrying her siblings to safety, one by one, from an unknown assailant.

"They'll all be sorry when I'm gone," she thought as she moved the knife closer. She could feel the point of the knife against her blouse. She closed her eyes, ready to thrust, but hesitated a moment. Then she opened her eyes, realizing she couldn't actually do it. With an agonizing sigh, she slowly took the knife from her chest and slipped it back into the drawer.

You may wonder what could be so bad to cause an outgoing seventeen-year-old to want to end her life. No one could see the pain. No one could see the pressure. Pressure to achieve because her older brother with so much potential had dropped out of high school. Pressure to be a "good big sister" to five adopted siblings. Pressure to replace her sister who had died a few years earlier. Pressure to be the perfect daughter for her workaholic father.

I know. I lived it. *I* was that girl. I'm glad I put the knife back in the drawer that day. Had I been successful in my suicide attempt, however, no one would have known why.

No one could see my pain because I hid it so well. I wanted to make everything right for everyone. I thought that was my job. With no one to talk to, my pain turned inward and caused illness and depression.

In 1971 I came to Christ, and over the next three years, he dealt with my depression, loneliness, anger, and insecurities. Since then, I've had very few bouts with depression. Nearly thirty years have passed, and I can count on two hands the number of hours I've been depressed.

I'll share some of the things God did to help me heal, but first, I'd like to introduce you to Ann. She's someone I admire who's also been able to deal with her past and move on.

ANN

"As a child, I would daydream about marriage. I'd picture a couple arguing and fighting. They'd be screaming and throwing things. Then somehow they'd resolve the conflict, and everything would be peaceful for a time. That's what I thought marriage was like."

Ann is the oldest of five children. Her father was in the army, and consequently, gone a lot. When she was five, her parents divorced after only seven years of marriage. Ann's mother was a caring person, but she got into a life of drugs. When Ann was seven, her mother was arrested and sent to prison.

All five children went to live with their grandmother. From there they were passed back and forth between relatives and friends. When Ann turned eight, her dad returned from Germany and took all his children with him to Texas, where he married a woman with six children of her own.

"That's when the sexual abuse started. I think my dad abused my younger sister, too, and possibly even my stepsisters. No one ever talked about it. It's still a 'non-subject' to this day."

When she turned twelve, Ann's mom, now out of jail, sent airplane tickets to her children to visit her in California. She had married a man with three children. In addition, she had another child by another man and one with her new husband. Ten kids in all, with Ann the oldest. There wasn't any money to buy tickets back to Texas, so they remained in California with their mom.

Ann's mom was still heavily into drugs and would often pass out on the sofa. Ann was the designated "nurse" and spent many hours caring for her mom. In an attempt to protect her children, Ann's mom taught them how to buy the "right" kind of drugs and even offered to get them whatever they wanted. Ann decided to take her mother up on the offer.

By age sixteen, Ann was so unhappy and disgusted with her mother's lifestyle that she ran away from home. She was arrested for shoplifting and sent to jail for a few days. This was the first time Ann had been caught, even though she'd been stealing for many years. Her entire code of ethics consisted of two rules: Don't steal from your friends, and don't snitch.

The police gave Ann the choice of going home or going back to jail. She chose jail. That's when she ended up in a foster home.

"My foster mom was an extremely dominant and controlling person," Ann admits. "It was exactly what I needed. I got off drugs and began to change a lot of my bad habits." During this time, Ann started to get sexually involved with guys. "I was looking for that perfect relationship. I knew I'd never get married because good marriages weren't possible."

At nineteen, Ann joined the army. Her promiscuous lifestyle continued. She justified it by convincing herself she was "in love."

Then at age twenty-one, Ann came to Christ. The big difference was that she now felt guilty about her lifestyle. In fact, one of her boyfriends said, "You used to be a really fun, carefree person, but you're so full of guilt now."

She continued on her guilt-ridden merry-go-round until she got involved in a good church. There she received counseling and began to heal. She was also able to deal with some of the issues from her childhood.

Soon she realized her merry-go-round was caused in part by her view of sin. "I thought Christians had this superhuman type of resistance to sin," she admits. "I'd get together with an old boyfriend, thinking I could resist because I had this invisible shield around me. I was so confused when I would end up in bed with him. I was ashamed and confused and defeated. My lowest point came when I started my first day of Bible school thinking I was pregnant. The inconsistencies were awful."

A light came on when her pastor talked to her about fleeing temptation—not embracing it. "If you're on a diet, don't go to the donut shop," he told her. It was a truth that helped transform her life.

Her thinking and behavior finally began to change as she immersed herself in God's Word and principles. Did you catch that? She *immersed* herself in God's Word and principles. From that point on, by God's grace, she was able to remain pure until she got married.

It was an unlikely match. Ann was twenty-eight when she met Robert. He'd come over to fix the roof of the house Ann was living in. They started talking and found an ease with one another. "I think I was almost the first female Robert ever had a conversation with. He was very shy," says Ann. Before long, Robert asked her out.

She decided she'd go out once, but that was all. She was headed to the mission field. Robert was deeply rooted in Oregon.

After the first date, she headed straight for her pastor's office. "I don't know what to do. He's such a nice guy, but he has no interest in missions. Am I being unfaithful to God?" she asked. They discussed the pros and cons, and he suggested she give it eight weeks. She did. Seven months later they were married.

"I never thought I'd marry a guy like Robert. He was pure; I'd been about as promiscuous as a person can get. He was from a stable home; I wasn't. He was close to his siblings; I wasn't. In fact, I'd listen to people talk about the kind of person you *shouldn't* marry—someone who'd been into drugs, sex, alcohol, and so on. I was all those things and more. I was the kind of person no one should marry. That never made sense to me, but I felt like I was damaged goods. I'm grateful Robert was able to overlook my past."

Robert and Ann wanted to start their marriage with as much positive input as possible. They took every opportunity available for premarital counseling. Their pastor was alarmed about a temperament analysis test they took.

"Robert was off the charts passive, and I was off the charts dominant," Ann admits. "I was extremely social; Robert was extremely quiet. It seemed like there was nothing in the middle—it was all extreme. But our pastor was willing to work with us. We learned so much from him that has helped us in our marriage. When we'd come up against a problem, I'd remember what my pastor had said and think, 'We were warned about this,' and we were able to solve it without a lot of conflict. It was amazing!"

Because of great premarital counseling and tender, teachable hearts, Robert and Ann not only have a great marriage, but they also have a stable home for their children—something Ann never expected. Her childhood daydreams (nightmares, really) of marriage haven't come true, and no one is more grateful than she.

Working through your past can be difficult and seem impossible at times. Yet, those who choose to face it head-on rather than evade it are able to heal more quickly and move on.

When I was in the seventh grade, I stepped on a nail. It was bleeding pretty heavily, and we weren't at home, so my mom put a bandage on it. By the time we got home, it had stopped bleeding, so we left it alone. The next morning I had a funny-looking bump on the top of my foot that hurt like crazy. My mom decided a doctor should look at it. The doctor wasn't sure what was wrong but decided he needed to open the wound and find out. I have a pretty high tolerance to pain, but it was excruciating when he cut into my foot, even with novocaine. He discovered that when I stepped on the nail, a small part of the rubber from my tennis shoe had been pushed into my foot. He had to dig out the rubber before my foot could heal properly.

That's often what we do with pain in our lives. We put a bandage on it because we don't want it to bleed all over everything. The problem is, it always surfaces and in any number of ways—sometimes in anger or overly-controlling behavior or eating disorders, or, as in my case, illness and depression.

If we would learn to face problems when they arise, they would be much less painful. I could have said to the doctor, "Excuse me, but this is too painful. I think I'd like to leave the rubber where it is." He could have let me keep the rubber in my foot, but what would have happened? It would have gotten worse, and the procedure would have been more painful and more difficult. Eventually, I would have lost my foot—talk about pain! Or perhaps my leg! In the end, if I'd done nothing, I would have lost my life—all because I didn't want to experience pain.

Pain tells us there's something wrong. It simply points out what is already there that needs to be dealt with. I urge you to deal with issues as the Lord brings them to your attention. If you can't face them alone, find a professional you trust to help you work through them. A professional can help you discern if your difficulty is something from the past that needs to be dealt with on an emotional level or if it's some kind of chemical deficiency that needs to be treated medically.

The past doesn't have to control your future. Robert and Ann wouldn't be married today if they had continued to live in the past.

What if Robert had been the kind of man who refused to allow his wife to live for today and kept reminding her of her past, constantly bringing up the fact that she wasn't pure when they married? Or what if Ann had been unable to allow her husband to be the person he is because she put all men in the same category? (If anyone has the right to be down on men, it's Ann.) Yet Robert and Ann refused to let their past control their marriage.

If Alan and I lived in the past, we wouldn't be married right now. We had so much going against us. Between the two of us—just our immediate families—parents and siblings—there are thirteen divorces. We had no models of good marriages to point us in the right direction. We came to Christ when we were in our early twenties, just months before we got married. We had no clue what it took to have a good marriage. It took us about ten years to work through most of our differences and learn how to communicate in a productive way. Many of the principles in this book come from what we learned those first ten years. Hopefully, our mistakes will help you have an awesome marriage.

Jesus said, "I have come that they may have life, and that they may have it more abundantly" (John 10:10 NKJV). In the New Living Translation we read, "My purpose is to give life in all its fullness." God wants us to have a full and abundant life, not just an existence.

When we live in light of our deficiencies (i.e., upbringing), we become trapped in the past. I'm not making light of the pain. It's real. I know that. But when we allow that pain to keep us victims, we lose out on what God has for our futures. We may have been victims in the past, but we're responsible for how we respond and react to that past. Remember, our past doesn't have to control or determine our future. We don't have to get stuck. We can take several steps to put the past behind and move on.

STEP ONE

First, we must ask God to show us the cause of our pain. Some of us have childhood traumas we've never addressed, which may include sexual, emotional, physical, or mental abuse, or a combination thereof. Any of these alone can cause enough pain to keep us victims forever. Perhaps we were involved in an accident in which someone was hurt or injured, or with drugs, alcohol, premarital sex, or any number of other things that cause pain. The list is really endless. That's why it's important to ask God to make the cause of our pain clear to us.

Fear, anger, depression, control, and manipulation are often used to cover up our pain. However, we're hurting ourselves more by not confronting the pain, and in most cases, we're also hurting our husbands and others in the process.

Most of us do everything we can to avoid pain, and we tend to do it in three ways. The first is a defense mechanism by which we come right up to pain, then at the last minute, go around it. As the pain increases, our desire to suffer through it decreases. We assume that we need to protect ourselves from pain, when, in fact, facing the pain is the beginning of the healing process.

The second way we avoid pain reminds me of a wind-up doll. You wind it and let it go. It moves just fine until it bumps into something. Then it turns around and goes the other way until it bumps into something else. So it goes until it runs out of gas. That's what many of us do when confronted with pain. We bump into it, but because it feels bad, we turn around and go the other way. Like the wind-up doll, we eventually run out of gas.

The third mechanism we use to avoid pain is to cover it up and pretend it's not there. Many of us would rather live with the fear of being found out than to face the pain.

Discovering the cause of pain is so difficult that sometimes a professional is needed to guide us through the steps and make sure we don't bypass anything that will help us on the road to recovery.

STEP TWO

The second step is to ask God to forgive us. Even if we are not responsible for the original offense(s), we *are* responsible for how we handle it. The anger you carry from the past is still sin no matter what the cause. Many of us think we're trapped in a family pattern. "Well, my parents were both screamers," we say, "and that's just the way we Smiths are. I can't help it. I come from a long line of screamers, and I've just learned to accept it." Sin is sin. I don't care where it comes from, and we must deal with it as such.

As a new wife, I found myself angry at Alan for every little thing. It seemed that almost anything would set me off. I wasn't sure why. I remember confessing my anger to God. On several occasions I knelt next to the bed and asked God to take away my anger. After several minutes the anger would dissolve. On my way to rejoin Alan, I'd feel the anger rise again. I'd turn around and go back to the bedroom where I'd again kneel and ask God to take my anger away. I continued this pattern until I could join Alan without the anger. Sometimes it would take minutes, and sometimes it would take hours.

A few years later, I came face-to-face with my anger. I don't really remember the circumstances, but I do remember how God used it to show me, in part, the cause of my anger. As I spent time reading my Bible, I realized I was angry at my parents. I was angry because I had to be so responsible. I was angry because they got a divorce. I was angry because my sister had died. I was angry because my dad was a workaholic. I was angry at a lot of things.

I was strongly convicted that the Lord wanted me to release all this anger. As I knelt and prayed, I asked him to forgive me for being angry. I gave him all my broken hopes and dreams. I gave him all my wishes for a different life. I basically gave him the right to choose my life and experiences. I asked him for the grace to accept the pain of my past and to move on to what he had for me in the future. Afterwards, I felt twenty pounds lighter. It was like a huge weight was lifted off my back. My bouts with depression disappeared. I won't say I've never gotten angry since then (you'd know I was lying), but I was free from the constant underlying anger.

When someone else causes us pain, the most unnatural thing to do is to forgive and forget. It's contrary to our desire to "get even." Neil

Andersen says, "Forgiveness is agreeing to live with the consequences of another person's sin."[1]

In Colossians 3:12–13 we read, "Since God chose you to be the holy people whom He loves, you must clothe yourselves with tenderhearted mercy, kindness, humility, gentleness, and patience. You must make allowance for each other's faults and forgive the person who offends you. Remember, the Lord forgave you, so you must forgive others."

Because forgiveness is so unnatural, it is extremely difficult. However, it's what God did for us. While we were shaking our fist at God, he forgave us. While we were nailing him to the cross, he forgave us. "While we were still sinners, Christ died for us" (Rom. 5:8 NIV).

STEP THREE

Once we ask God to show us the cause of our pain and seek his forgiveness, we can continue the healing process. Only God's supernatural power can bring total healing. Scripture is invaluable in the process. We must memorize portions that address our particular issues and think about their meaning throughout the day, especially when we're in the middle of a struggle. Romans 12 was so valuable to me as I began the process of healing, especially verses 1 and 2: "Therefore, I urge you, brothers, in view of God's mercy, to offer your bodies as living sacrifices, holy and pleasing to God—this is your spiritual act of worship. Do not conform any longer to the pattern of this world, but be transformed by the renewing of your mind" (NIV). Verse 2 in another translation reads, "Let God transform you into a new person by changing the way you think." Oswald Chambers said it this way: "Leave the Irreparable Past in His hands, and step out into the Irresistible Future with Him."[2]

Remember, we may have been victims in the past, but we're 100 percent responsible from now on. We don't need to live the present in light of our past. That's what Ann discovered, and that's what Alan and I discovered. God was faithful and gave us the desire to know him and do what he says. That's the main reason we're still together today—and we enjoy an awesome relationship!

Chapter 3

COMPLETE,
DON'T COMPETE

To get a complete picture of a wife's role, we need to go back to creation. We have much to learn about relationships from the Genesis account of creation. After all, it was the beginning of relationships, and as we see the interaction between Adam and God and then Adam and Eve, we get a better view of God's original intention. Once the foundation is set, we can build the rest of our ideas from that.

As we picture Adam in the garden before Eve was created, we find something missing. I'm sure Adam was pleased with all he saw. Beauty surrounded him. The world was peaceful and serene, with sunshine during the day and the stars at night. The plants must have been gorgeous—the flowers beyond belief. It was literally paradise. Many animals of differing sizes and shapes abounded, and Adam's job was to name them. I would imagine that took quite a while, although not as long as if Eve had been there.

When I was pregnant with our first child, we struggled to find just the right name. We didn't know if we were having a boy or girl, so of course, we had to have two names. I'd suggest a name; it would remind Alan of someone he disliked, so we'd discard it. He'd suggest a name, and I'd look at him like he was nuts. He liked unusual names (I suppose it's a good thing or he may never have married me). He loved the name Montana for a girl. Can you imagine Montana Hlavka? I convinced him that our child needed a normal first name to counteract the difficulty she'd encounter with her last name. I knew from personal experience—first dealing with the name Theda Pranke and then Theda Hlavka. We ended up with a beautiful daughter named Joy Alison Hlavka.

Our second child was even more difficult to name. I was positive we were having a boy, so we didn't even pick out a girl's name. You can imagine our surprise when our second daughter was born. Alan liked the name Heather, and I liked the name Jennifer. It took us three days to agree on Heather Jennifer, thinking we could decide later what to call her. We call her Hessie.

Our third daughter was a surprise, but not in the usual way. We had been trying to adopt for about a year and a half when the case-worker called and said, "We have a child for you. A three-day-old girl, and if you want her, she has to be picked up from the hospital before five o'clock." Months earlier, we'd been told to expect a boy around the age of six, so not only did we have to pick her up, but we needed to name her (not to mention having no clothes, crib, car seat, etc.). And now there were four of us to name her. On the way to sign the papers and pick up our precious little daughter, we finally settled on naming her after a close friend whom we greatly admire, Karen Jean.

We only needed three names. Adam had countless animals to name. It probably took all the creative powers he had. I imagine some were more difficult than others, but when it came to naming the person God created just for him, he had no trouble at all.

God created the heavens and the earth (Gen. 1:1); then he created day and night (vv. 3–5). He saw that it was good. Next he created the sky (vv. 6–8). Then he separated the water from the land and saw that it was good (vv. 9–10). Next he created all kinds of plants. "And God saw that it was good" (vv. 11–13). Then he created the sun and the moon and the stars (vv.14–19), the water and sky (vv. 20–23), and all the animals (vv. 24–25). Lastly, he created man (v. 26). Every step of creation, God concluded that his handiwork was good. This is very important because in Genesis 2:18, "The LORD God said, 'It is not good for the man to be alone; I will make him a helper suitable for him'" (NASB). Did you catch that? It was *not* good.

Perhaps God was creating a desire in Adam for a mate as he brought the animals to him to name. I'm sure that Adam couldn't help but notice that each animal had another of its kind, similar, but different. But there was no creature for Adam. Genesis 2:20 states, "But for Adam there was not found a helper comparable to him" (NKJV).

Why not? Didn't God create incredible creatures? What about a dog? Dogs are "man's best friend," aren't they? Couldn't a dog fill the void? Or what about another man? Someone to do "guy" things with—like watching football or Arnold Schwarzeneggar movies or going hunting or fishing. Why couldn't another guy fill the void?

Elisabeth Elliot said, "But Adam needed more than the companionship of the animals or the friendship of a man. He needed a helper, specially designed and prepared to fill that role. It was a woman God gave him."[1]

God deliberately created a void in the man and chose a woman to fill that void. Notice that he didn't create a void in the woman. This is significant.

God's intention from the very beginning was that man would not be complete in and of himself. He fashioned woman to be the man's helper, to fit his needs exactly—physically, emotionally, spiritually, and mentally. This is a very profound truth. It may also be a truth that rubs you the wrong way. We don't know why God did this, but we do know that our value to God is the same as that of a man. The term *helper* is used about God himself. In Hebrews 13:6 we read, "The LORD is my helper; I will not fear. What can man do to me?" (NKJV). In John 14:16, "And I will pray the Father, and He will give you another Helper, that He may abide with you forever—the Spirit of truth" (NKJV). And John 15:26 reads, "But when the Helper comes, whom I shall send to you from the Father, the Spirit of truth who proceeds from the Father, He will testify of Me" (NKJV). I don't find that demeaning, do you?

The word *helper* is defined as "someone who contributes strength." Imagine a string quartet. It consists of four different instruments— generally two violins, a viola, and a cello. They work together to make a beautiful sound.

Recently, a friend came into my kindergarten music class to demonstrate her cello to the students. It's a rather large instrument and somewhat bulky to carry, but when Susan began to play a piece of music, the children were enthralled. They were even more enthralled when she played "Old MacDonald," "Twinkle, Twinkle, Little Star," and the theme from *Jaws*. You should have seen the smiles and giggles when they each got a turn to play.

As fun as that was (and it was great fun), and as beautifully as Susan played (and she played beautifully), it was nothing compared to hearing the intricacies and harmonies of a string quartet, with each instrument contributing its own special strength to the others. Of course, if each musician chose to "do his own thing" and play whatever he "felt led" to play, it would be total chaos, similar to what takes place as musicians in an orchestra tune up before they begin to play. It's not a pretty sound. However, if each member uses a master plan (musical score), he will reproduce what the composer had in mind when he wrote the music—a beautiful display of creativity. This is what God had in mind when he created a woman to fill the void in Adam's life.

In marriage, *helper* doesn't mean inferior, just as a cello isn't inferior or superior to a violin or a viola or any other instrument. It's a part of the whole—a part that would be sorely missed if it were gone. Being a helper has nothing to do with who's stronger or smarter or more gifted or anything else. It has *only* to do with God's plan.

The Scriptures contain a number of passages I don't particularly like. I don't like "dying to self" or "taking up my cross" or "choosing between God and money" or "offering myself as a living sacrifice," but I do it because that's what God's plan is for me. A surprising thing happens when I live my life the way God intended and by his Spirit. I am fulfilled, content, and joyful. The same is true when I understand my unique role as a woman.

A young woman is sitting and waiting. She isn't quite twenty-one. She's been waiting for more than an hour for the second day in a row. Her husband of only three weeks is late again. "Where could he be?" she asks their small black dachshund. "He promised he'd be on time today." She can feel her anger rising as she recalls their conversation from the day before.

"A few kids stayed after school to play catch with the football." As he had said this yesterday, jealousy raged through her. She had seen some of the "kids" at the high school where he worked—beautiful young girls with long blond hair.

"But I've been waiting for you for over an hour," she whined. In fact, she had been waiting for him all day. New in town, she had no friends. He had their only car, so she spent most of her day reading magazines, watching television, and talking to the dog.

He had promised her he'd come straight home after work from then on. But here she was again, waiting. She checked the clock for the tenth time, her anger rising. An hour and fifteen minutes. Her imagination ran wild. *Those young girls are after him; I just know it. He's probably eating it up,* she thought. She didn't trust her handsome young husband. Why should she? All men were alike. Her father had left her mother for a younger woman just weeks earlier. She was convinced her husband would do the same thing.

Finally she hears the car. She picks up a magazine, pretending to read. As he enters, she stands. "Where have you been?" she accuses. "I'm sorry I'm late," he says. "You won't believe what happened. I stopped for a train on the way home, but the guy behind me didn't. He rear-ended me and pushed me into the path of an oncoming train. The train hit the front of the car, and I could barely drive it home. You should see it; it's a mess." Unable to control her frustration and anger, she blurts out, "Do you know what that's going to do to our insurance?" As she turns to pick up her magazine, she misses the look on his face. He wonders why he even tries.

That isn't exactly the scenario of a woman who completes her husband. I'm ashamed to say that was me some thirty years ago. I've grown up a lot since then, and by God's grace, I've also grown in my ability to be a helper and not a hindrance to my husband.

Take a look at a similar situation just a few years ago. Dinner's been ready for some time. He called an hour ago to say he was on his way. "Where's your father?" she asks their youngest child, now twelve, as she passes through on her way to the bedroom. "I thought he was on his way," the child mumbles. "Yeah, but that was an hour ago." After all, the trip from the office should take ten minutes or less. She wonders if she should call someone who might know where he is. She decides to wait a few more minutes. Soon she hears his car. She runs to open the door and turn the light on for him. "Are you all right?" she asks. "Sorry I'm late. Steve grabbed me just as I was leaving, and we ended up in a long conversation." Relief washes over her: "That's all right; I'm just glad you're OK." Same situation. Same two characters, but different responses. God is gracious and "grows us up" as we're able and willing to follow him.

THE CURSE

In chapter 3 of Genesis, we read about the fall of man (and woman) and God's curse on them. If you will notice, even though Eve was the one who ate the fruit and then convinced Adam to eat it (she probably used woman's ultimate line, "You never like anything I fix."), he is the one who had to answer to God. Why? God has chosen man to be ultimately responsible. Unfortunately, Adam tried to avoid that responsibility by blaming Eve. She, in turn, blamed the serpent. Not much has changed, has it?

I find God's curse on the woman very revealing. "To the woman he said, 'I will greatly increase your pains in childbearing; with pain you will give birth to children. Your desire will be for your husband, and he will rule over you'" (Gen. 3:16 NIV).

I can attest to the childbearing part. Our firstborn took fifteen hours of labor and would have taken a lot longer if the doctor hadn't used forceps to deliver her. Our second daughter was delivered by C-section, which was no picnic either. Adoption is definitely the way to go. I ran three miles the day Karen was born! And no doubt, you're aware that when a group of young mothers gets together, the conversation often drifts toward labor and delivery stories. It ends up being a kind of "can you top this horror story?" festival.

What about the other part of the curse? What is that all about? What exactly does it mean that her desire is for her husband? It's what we're seeing a lot of in today's society.

Women don't want men telling them what to do. They want to tell men what to do. They want to be the bosses. Now don't get me wrong here. Women have made many positive strides in the last one hundred years, including the right to vote. Can you believe that in 1905 Grover Cleveland was quoted as saying, "Sensible and responsible women do not want to vote"? Men have long been ruling in an unbiblical fashion. The oppression of women has been severe at times. No one has the right to treat another human being the way some men have treated women over the centuries and continue to do all over the world.

However, I believe the current trend has gone too far the other way. Women are acting out the curse of Genesis 3. Their desire is to rule over their husbands, much as men have been doing over women for centuries, which is wrong. Remember, it's the curse, not the intention of God.

I believe women have been trying to usurp their husbands' authority since the beginning. You only need to look a few chapters further in Genesis and see where Sarah convinces Abraham to lie for her, sleep with her maid, and banish his own son by that maid. Proverbs has many examples of women who were less than fun to live with. "It is better to live alone in the corner of an attic than with a contentious wife in a lovely home" (Prov. 21:9). The Bible has many other examples, but you get the point. You probably know women like this—you may even be this kind of woman. If so, you're living out the curse.

We can overcome the desire to rule over our husbands because "greater is he that is in you than he that is in the world" (1 John 4:4 KJV). God has given us the resources to be the "suitable helper" he created us to be. We can begin by realizing our God-given responsibility.

Many women aren't even aware of God's plan for them. Once they re-alize it and commit themselves to doing whatever God calls them to do, half the battle is already won. I believe that the main responsibility of a wife is to show respect to her husband.

In Ephesians 5:33, we read, "So again I say, each man must love his wife as he loves himself, and the wife must respect her husband." This directive isn't based on whether he's doing a good job or not. It's based on the fact that God commands us to do it.

The Amplified Bible reads, "and let the wife see that she respects and reverences her husband—that she notices him, regards him, hon-ors him, prefers him, venerates and esteems him; and that she defers to him, praises him, and loves and admires him exceedingly."

Wow! Can you imagine the man whose wife does all this? There's something deep inside a man that needs this kind of affirmation from the one person who knows him best. I believe the need is God-given.

Amy and Rick have been married for almost ten years. They have a great marriage. This is due partly to the fact that they were best friends before they realized they wanted to spend the rest of their lives together.

"I feel like we're a good team," says Amy. "Rick is such a servant-hearted and giving person. It makes me want to give back to him, which creates an atmosphere where we enjoy doing things for each other" (see Rom. 12:10).

Amy claims that her greatest problem is being patient and letting Rick take the initiative. "I've learned that Rick takes time to process things. I tend to want a quick answer. It would be easy for me to take over. What I *try* to do is give my opinion and then wait for Rick to work it through. We really don't argue much, especially when I take this approach. I have to work hard not to overpower him and allow him time to think about and process it. Rick values my opinion and listens to me. I try not to abuse that."

She says, "Rick's greatest need is to feel respected. I have the ability with my attitude to build him up or tear him down. When I show him

I respect him, it gives him the confidence to do what he needs to do. He often says I'm his biggest cheerleader. He knows I'm on his team and I'm pulling for him."

Each man is uniquely created by God and has different needs, hopes, and desires. Our job is to study and try to understand our own husband's unique needs and to complete, not compete, with them.

Carole is a dear friend of mine. As I observe her relationship with her husband, William, I'm impressed with the way she's put principles of affirmation into practice in her marriage.

William and Carole aren't perfect, and they've come to realize that a good marriage takes a lot of work—the kind of work most people aren't willing to do. Carole met William a few years after she and her first husband divorced. With two children in tow, she and William began their life together. Since it was the second marriage for both, they knew they'd have to work hard to keep theirs intact. Four years after they were married, they became Christians. It was a turning point for them, as they were now able to see their marriage from God's point of view.

They were determined to follow God's plan. It wasn't always easy, but as Carole committed herself to meeting William's unique needs, they eventually worked through most of their difficulties.

Carole strongly believes in valuing and esteeming her husband. "The little things are often the most important," she says. "It lets a man know you're thinking about him."

She also constantly builds him up in front of others. I have only heard positive things about William from Carole. Every time she sees him, she says something positive to or about him. I've heard things like, "Isn't he the cutest thing you've ever seen?"; "You're such a good guy"; "He's my rock"; "I don't know what I'd do without him"; and so on and so on and so on.

Carole also believes it's important to "notice" your husband. I once asked her what she meant by that and how she applied it. I was a little surprised by her answer. "I tell him what I like about him physically, and I tell him how sexy he is." Now that's a healthy relationship!

OK, now you're convinced that God wants you to "contribute strength" to your relationship. So what are you supposed to *do?*

1. Desire God's will more than your own. This principle applies not only to your relationship with your husband but to *every* part of your life. Desiring God's will is central to everything you do, think, or say. Mark 12:30 teaches us to "[l]ove the Lord your God with all your heart and with all your soul and with all your mind and with all your strength" (NIV). You must cultivate your relationship with the Lord the same way you cultivate a relationship with a good friend. Quality time is the key. As with any important friendship, you must spend time with God. A first step is to get involved in a good church. You also need to spend time reading your love letter from God (the Bible) and talking with him. Over time, your relationship with him will deepen and become your main focus.

2. Learn to adapt to your husband. Accomplishing this task is a very unnatural and difficult thing to do, especially because society teaches us to do the opposite. However, if you want to do God's will, this is it. In Philippians 2:4 we read, "Each of you should look not only to your own interests, but also to the interests of others" (NIV).

3. Realize that your husband does not belong to you but to God. "For you were bought at a price; therefore glorify God in your body and in your spirit, which are God's" (1 Cor. 6:20 NKJV).

4. Communicate. Good communication is essential to a healthy marriage. Without it, nothing will be accomplished. This topic will be further discussed in chapter 6.

As you rethink your role and apply principles from Scripture, you'll begin to get the big picture. Being a strength-contributor brings wonderful fulfillment and joy to marriage. We're not insignificant. What we do *does* matter—for eternity, and it just might renew our marriage.

Chapter 4

THE "S" WORD IS NOT *SLAVE*

*M*any years ago in the land of Odd lived a people with an unusual lifestyle. The women worked during the day while their husbands cleaned house and took care of the children. These women loved it because they'd work at the office all day and came home to a clean house and well-mannered children. Their main jobs in the evening were to eat a hearty dinner, prepared by their lovely husbands, put their feet up, watch television, and drink Diet Coke until bedtime.

Meanwhile, the men gave the children their baths, read to them, and tucked them into bed. They also cleaned the kitchen, washed and folded a few loads of laundry, scrubbed the entry, vacuumed, dusted, then fell into bed at eleven o'clock. That's when their wives were finished watching television and would expect "a little action" from their exhausted husbands. Even though they had no energy or interest after such a tiring day, the men knew it was their "duty" to meet their wives' sexual needs.

This went on for many years until one day the husbands all got together for coffee. As they began talking, they decided they were tired of doing all the work while their wives sat around getting Diet Coke bellies. The more they talked the angrier they got, until finally they decided to confront their wives and tell them they weren't going to take it anymore.

Well, you can imagine that the confrontation didn't set well with the women, and they began scouring the Internet for help. They finally ran across a website with Bible verses in it. They skipped over everything they didn't like and found a verse that would put an end to this whole foolish men's rebellion. It said, "Husbands, submit to your wives as to the Lord. For the wife is the head of the husband as Christ is the head of the church, his body, of which he is the Savior. Now as the church submits to Christ, so also husbands should submit to their wives in everything."

When the wives read this passage to their husbands, the men sighed a collective sigh of resignation and went back to their husbandly duties, and they all lived happily ever after—at least the women did.

Why does this sound so ludicrous? For one thing, men could never do all that work and live to tell about it. Another is, women have been doing this for years. We read that wives are to submit to their husbands, throw up their hands in resignation, and live absolutely miserable lives. Is this what God expects? Is this what he wants? Is this what the Bible really teaches?

I think part of the problem with the idea of submission is that we've lost sight of our real purpose. First and foremost, we are to love the Lord our God with all our heart, mind, soul, and strength. Then, as we've already seen in Genesis, we're to complete our husbands—adding our strength to theirs. We get mired down in things that make no sense because we're trying to do the third thing first. We try to make sense of submission when we haven't first "chosen what is better," that is, sitting at the feet of Jesus.

Before we can address the submission issue, we must come to grips with the second reason we're on this earth—to fill the God-created void in man. Then and only then does submission make sense. Our husband's mission is to be first and foremost, and ours is to be a *sub-mission*. What is our husband's mission? His first is the same as ours—to love the Lord with all his heart, mind, soul, and strength. Then he's to love his wife as Christ loved the church and to give himself up for her. Then he's to multiply a godly legacy (through children). Is your husband weak when it comes to loving God? Or loving you? Or training your children? Then you know what your submission is.

As we evaluate our roles, we need to take a look from God's perspective. Notice that God calls us to be helpers, not slaves. Submission is something we do, not something we are. Helper is something we are. That's our role in the relationship.

"Wives, submit to your husbands as to the Lord. For the husband is the head of the wife as Christ is the head of the church, his body, of which he is the Savior. Now as the church submits to Christ, so also wives should submit to their husbands in everything" (Eph. 5:22–24 NIV).

Ladies, this is not a drudgery. It's life-giving and God-honoring. It's funny to me that we look at this passage and others and have such a hard time with them. Look at all the things a husband is supposed to do. Verses 25–33 are all about how a husband is to love his wife. He's to love her as Christ loved the church and as his own body. He's to give himself up for her. He's to nourish her, present her without stain, wrinkle, or blemish—holy and blameless. It's an impossible task. On the other hand, only three verses are addressed to the wife in this passage, verses 22, 24, and the last part of 33.

We have a distorted view of what submission is. We often think of it as being part of a hierarchy, similar to the military. God is first, man is second, and the wife is last. This perspective often looks like the husband being the drill sergeant and the wife being the "yessir" private. Whatever he says, I do—no questions asked.

On the other hand, many of us discount submission altogether and go for the world's 50/50 plan, which says, "I'll do my half if you do yours." It's a great idea, but it rarely works. How do you know when you've done your 50 percent? What if your idea of 50 percent is different from his?

Most couples who use this plan end up with one spouse doing more work than the other. And what about affection? How do you know when you've given 50 percent of the affection? Or money? Does that mean each person has to earn the same amount? Do you take turns mowing the lawn? Or taking out the garbage? Or vacuuming? Or . . . or . . . or—you get the point.

The way God intends marriage to work is through partnership and cooperation. Remember, men and women have equal value in God's eyes, but God has given us each different roles. Both Alan and I give 100 percent to the relationship.

Jesus was God in human form. He was totally God and totally man at the same time. In Philippians 2:5–8 we read, "Your attitude should be the same as that of Christ Jesus: Who, being in very nature God, did not consider equality with God something to be grasped, but made himself nothing, taking the very nature of a servant, being made in human likeness. And being found in appearance as a man, he humbled himself and became obedient to death—even death on a cross!" (NIV). He "submitted" his will to the will of the Father and died on the cross for you and me. Jesus didn't complain because he had to submit himself to the Father's will. They had determined together before the beginning of time that this would happen. Why would he have a problem with it?

Jesus' actions illustrate how we are to interact with our husbands. It's not wrong to determine together in which direction to go. We must pray together and seek God's will together. If it's a major issue (like where to live), it may take longer—more discussion, more prayer. If it's a relatively minor situation (like where to go to dinner), you can hash it out in a matter of minutes. No matter what the degree of the decision, the process is the same. Each spouse considers the other.

We also know that Jesus agonized over the manner of his death. If you look in the Garden of Gethsemane, you see a man in anguish. Why?

"They went to a place called Gethsemane, and Jesus said to his disciples, 'Sit here while I pray.' He took Peter, James and John along with him, and he began to be deeply distressed and troubled. 'My soul is overwhelmed with sorrow to the point of death,' he said to them. 'Stay here and keep watch.'

"Going a little farther, he fell to the ground and prayed that if possible the hour might pass from him. 'Abba, Father,' he said, 'everything is possible for you. Take this cup from me. Yet not what I will, but what you will'" (Mark 14:32–36 NIV).

Jesus was in agony. He begged his Father to get him out of the situation. What torture that must have been, but he chose to be "obedient to death—even death on a cross."

Don't miss the correlation here. It's alright to have an opinion and to express it stridently. Obviously there's no sin in that. Go ahead and let your husband know how you feel. Sometimes that may mean giving him time to process the information—perhaps for an hour, or even a day or two. Discuss it long and hard, but in the end, if he's not willing to change his mind, you must let him lead. If Jesus can follow the lead of the Father, then we're in pretty good company. Wouldn't you agree?

I've discovered that a woman's submission to her husband is rarely an issue in marriages where both husband and wife are living in submission to the Father's will. Alan and I can only think of half a dozen times when submission has even been an issue in our marriage.

One reason why submission is not an issue for us is because I made a choice when I first got married not to usurp Alan's authority. It would be quite simple for me to "rule over my husband" because I'm more strong-willed than Alan. He's a compliant person and tries hard to please. I know beyond the shadow of a doubt I could get my way 100 percent of the time and "appear" submissive. I know how to do it. However, I have chosen *not* to run everything because God doesn't want me to. Furthermore, when it comes right down to it, submission to my husband is really submission to God.

While submission is key to a godly marriage, being the helper or strength-giver in the relationship is more important. If we keep that in focus, submission isn't very often an issue.

As we live our lives in obedience to Christ, we give up many things. We give up pride, selfishness, anger, jealousy, gossip, and so forth. In return, we receive our helper, the Holy Spirit, and love, joy, peace, and so on. These aren't things we work for; they are gifts. As we live our lives in submission to God and by the power of the Holy Spirit, he replaces the old stuff with the new life, his life.

As we die to self, we are able and willing to do whatever God asks us to do. In fact, it becomes a pleasure and brings us true fulfillment. I believe that's why Paul and Silas were able to sing songs of praise while in prison and after being beaten.

WHAT SUBMISSION IS *NOT*

Let's get down to some specifics, shall we? Here are some things that submission is *not.*

- It is not blindly following your husband no matter what—especially if he isn't walking with the Lord. God gave you a brain, and he expects you to use it.
- Submission doesn't mean you have to lose who you are as a person. God made you unique and has a plan for your life that is unlike the plan for anyone else. If you follow the Lord and do his will, you will become a more whole human being than you've ever been. You will be more fulfilled, more joyful, and more content. Don't give up being you.
- If an action involves violating the law, it is not submission. It's *not* God's will for you to go against his will in order to submit to your husband. Please get some help immediately if this is your situation.
- You don't have to allow your husband to be physically, verbally, or sexually abusive in order to be submissive. Don't allow it! Please get help immediately!
- Submission does not involve a superior person and an inferior person. Remember, we are "one in Christ." Our roles are only that, roles, not worth. We walk and work side by

side, headed for the same goal. The husband is the loving servant-leader. The wife is the loving servant-helper.

WHAT SUBMISSION *IS*

What, then, *does* submission mean?

- The husband is to lay down his life for his wife as Christ laid down his life for the church. The wife is to love, honor, and respect her husband as the church loves, honors, and respects Christ.

  Together the husband and wife mirror the image of God, presenting a picture to the world of who God is. A good marriage is truly a miracle in today's world.

- A submissive wife encourages her husband to lead. Many men will let their wives handle everything because it involves less work and emotional pain. Their wives don't trust them to do a good job. I have a friend who will let her husband do very little around the house because he doesn't do it right. So what? Would you rather have an efficiently run house or a biblically sound marriage? Unfortunately, many of us would choose the house. This is due, in part, to the fact that we haven't really given up our whole lives to God. We're not willing to follow no matter the cost, including a perfect house. That's not only sad, it's wrong.

Several years ago I realized I wasn't allowing Alan to have much say in raising our girls. I wasn't aware of it until he pointed it out. Whenever they needed something or wanted to go somewhere, they'd ask me, not Alan. Once I realized what was happening, I started to turn it back over to him. When the girls would come to me, I'd say, "Go ask Dad." He'd get my input and then make a decision. I never realized how freeing that would be. Not only did I still have as much input as I ever had, but I didn't have to rely only on my wisdom (or lack of it). Furthermore, if the girls disagreed with the decision, I didn't have to take the brunt of it. After all, it was Dad who told them no. It was a great weight off my shoulders because the final authority of the matter was where it belonged, with Alan, the head of the household.

- Submission also honors God. I want with all my heart to bring honor to God, and submitting to my husband is a tangible way I can do that—"being subject to their own husbands, that the word of God may not be dishonored" (Titus 2:5b NASB). Sometimes I struggle with knowing exactly what God wants me to do. In this area I have no doubts.

Kay has been married twenty years. She has done a great job living out the principles of honor and submission. (You'll learn more about her in chapter 10.) "The world tells us to follow its 50/50 plan. But God tells us we must give 100 percent all the time, no matter what our spouse does. There is no other way to make a marriage work," says Kay.

Kay does give 100 percent. "In my marriage," she says, "my job is to complement and complete Joe. God gave me certain insights and abilities Joe doesn't have many times. He *needs* my influence in order to make good decisions."

What if she doesn't agree with what Joe decides? "There are times we go head-to-head on an issue," says Kay. "I don't believe submission means blind obedience. If I don't agree, I let him know. If we still don't agree, I give him more input. He has a hard time compromising. Then if we still don't agree, I submit to his God-given authority. Just because I disagree doesn't mean I have to have my own way.

"Sometimes I come away with hurt feelings. I could stew and fret and throw a tantrum like many women I know, but I choose to deal with it and not hold a grudge. In marriage, you have to be very forgiving. I work hard at not grumbling or nagging.

"I have learned to be content with little answers to prayer—little victories. I have learned to have high hopes but low expectations. I keep my perspective by keeping a journal and reviewing it periodically to see progress I might otherwise overlook. I can see how things have improved. It's very encouraging.

"My responsibility and pleasure is to do all I can for my husband—not as his servant, but because I delight in serving him. I'm his closest friend. I must choose whether I will build him up or break him down. The world does a lot to break him down; I don't need to do it too. I don't focus on his weaknesses. I work hard at being careful how I say things—by my wording and tone of voice. He needs to feel I'm behind him, rooting for him. He needs my encouragement."

- Submission looks different in every home. I wish I could give you a list of do's and don'ts so you'd know exactly what to do, but I can't. A quiet man and a strong woman will have a totally different view of submission than a couple where both are strong I think God did it this way to keep us on our knees.

  Robert wants only to please Ann. Nothing gives him greater pleasure. "Sometimes I have to submit two or three times on the same issue just to find out what Robert *really* thinks," Ann says.

It is crucial to keep the right perspective—to realize we're here to glorify God. Apart from this, nothing matters. Ruth Myers, in her book *The Perfect Love*, outlines her life's primary goals. I have adopted them for myself; you might consider doing the same. "I think of my primary goals as these: I want to know God better and love Him more. I want to worship him the way He deserves. I want to do His will. And I want to glorify Him in all I am and say and do." [1]

We're not here to fulfill some dream of ours or even to find happiness, but to glorify the One who deserves our all—and nothing less. "All who claim me as their God will come, for I have made them for my glory. It was I who created them" (Isa. 43:7).

Chapter 5

YOU HAVE TO BE BILINGUAL TO TALK TO A MAN

"What time will you be home tonight?" she asked.

"The usual," her executive husband answered. "Do you know where my blue tie is?"

"In the closet, under your green one," she replied. "The usual-usual or the late-usual?"

"I looked, but it's not there," he said with frustration in his voice.

"Right here," she replied as she handed it to him.

"Thanks," he mumbled.

"The usual-usual or the late-usual?" she asked again.

"What?"

"I said, the usual-usual or the late-usual?" she replied.

"I have no idea what you're talking about," he said.

"Well, sometimes you come home at the usual-usual time, which is pretty rare, but it's really the time you're supposed to be home." She took a quick breath. "Then there's the late-usual, which is when you normally come home, and I was just wondering which one it's going to be tonight. The usual-usual or the late-usual?"

"I still have no idea what you're talking about," he said as he turned to look at her.

"Well, you see," she began, "you're *supposed* to work from nine to five, right?"

"What does that have to do with *anything*?"

"Well, when we first moved here, you were *supposed* to work from nine to five, which means you should get home between five-thirty and six, depending on traffic," she said, warming up to her subject.

He glanced at his watch. "Honey, could we finish this tonight? I really have to go."

"Sure, but when will you be home?" she asked for the third time.

"The usual," he said as he headed out the door.

The difficulty with communication is the misconception that it has taken place when in fact it hasn't. We think we're communicating, but all we're really doing is talking. Communication doesn't take place until the person we're speaking with understands the meaning of the words we're saying. We assume that because we speak words that make sense to us, the other person understands what we're trying to say, when in fact, the other person has no clue.

Whenever two imperfect human beings begin talking, they will have difficulty communicating. For instance, someone who uses his hands a lot when he talks has a more difficult time understanding someone who doesn't. Someone raised in a loud family could drive a quiet person crazy. Many factors contribute to the way we communicate—backgrounds, temperaments, experiences, gender, even vocabulary.

BACKGROUND

It's no problem for me to have several things going on at once and still carry on a conversation. I think that's partly due to the fact that I grew up in a family of nine, where lots of noise and several conversations often going on at once were commonplace. Alan, on the other hand, was alone a lot growing up and needs focused attention to carry on any kind of meaningful conversation.

TEMPERAMENT

I have a short attention span, so I need to know the bottom line at the beginning in order to track what the other person is saying. Otherwise, I have trouble understanding the purpose of the conversation. Alan, however, loves detail and tends to go off on rabbit trails when telling a story.

GENDER

Men and women generally don't communicate in the same way. Duh! Anyone who's been married for more than five minutes has discovered this. It doesn't mean one is right and the other wrong; it just means they're different.

For instance, most women have had a close relationship with at least one other woman at some point in their lives. It could have been (or still is) a mom, a sister, a roommate—someone they've communicated with on a heart level. In fact, sometimes the relationship is so close that neither one has to say anything to communicate. They pick up on what the other is thinking and feeling without ever uttering a word.

Men don't usually communicate like that. It's not that they can't; it's just that they never have and don't know how to because they've never been given the opportunity.

So, if a woman comes into marriage expecting to communicate with her man like she communicates with her female friends, she will most likely be disappointed.

Communication is foundational to a good marriage. Most of what we do hinges on transparency—whether we can share our true thoughts and ideas with our husbands in a way that assures we are being understood. A woman who's used to having someone read her thoughts would probably become frustrated with a man who needs to have everything spelled out word for word in bold letters.

It's like asking a cat to communicate with a bird. The bird may want to, but he has no way of doing it. "How can I communicate with that cat?" he asks. "What should I do? What should I say? And after all, she might be dangerous." The cat may want to communicate, but she has no way of letting the bird know she's not going to eat him. She thinks that if she purrs and paces a lot he'll get the picture. And so they continue their relationship, with the bird flying around, afraid to land, and the cat purring and pacing, hoping the bird will get the idea.

So it is in our relationships. The wife assumes her husband will pick up on her nonverbal messages. To her they're very clear—anyone should know what she's trying to say. The husband, however, often has had no training in this form of communication. His nonverbal antennae are bent or missing, so he assumes everything is great and that she'll tell him if something's wrong. She gets more and more frustrated while he is unaware anything is wrong, which makes her even more frustrated.

Soon she explodes in anger, "You don't love me!" He has no clue, so he does what he thinks will bring him closer to a solution. He asks, "What have I done now?" This infuriates her more, for two reasons. One, she assumes he's implying she does this all the time, which, of course, she does not! Two, she's positive he knows exactly what he's done, but he won't admit it.

And so it goes. Whether verbal or nonverbal, they can't seem to communicate. The problem is, they need to learn to speak each other's languages. The goal of communication is intimacy (or oneness). Therefore, communication goes beyond understanding what couples say to each other. They need to understand what each person *means.* Of course, this is easier said than done.

The root of the word *communication* is the word *common.* A commune is shared living. Communism is a shared economy. Communion is a shared Lord and fellowship. A community is a shared locale. Communication is a shared understanding.

The goal is to understand what the other person is saying. This does not mean the couple always agrees, but it will mean understanding the same information in the same way. If you understand the meaning behind what I say, we have communicated.

Dennis Rainey, in his book *Staying Close,* writes, "Nothing is as easy as talking; and nothing is as difficult as communicating."[1]

One additional point: Communication won't happen unless couples can trust each other. All healthy relationships are built on trust. Part of that trust means that you are safe to express how you feel without fearing rejection or ridicule.

We will now look at five levels of communication. Our goal as wives is to eventually get all the way to the fifth level with our husbands.

1. *Cliché* communication allows us to remain safely isolated and alone. It's restricted to greetings and comments that express no opinions, feelings, or real information.
2. *Fact* communication consists only of the objective discussion of facts. At this level you can still keep each other at arms length.
3. *Opinion* communication involves sharing ideas and opinions that will open your husband up as he expresses what he really thinks. This is where we can begin to open up to one another.
4. *Emotional* communication involves sharing feelings and emotions, which leads to true communication. It involves conveying your hopes, fears, likes, dislikes, disappointments, joys, sorrows, needs, dreams, failures, desires, stresses, and burdens. The walls begin to come down, and the heart starts to get exposed.
5. *Transparent* communication involves complete emotional and personal truthfulness. Transparency is sharing your heart. Before you can share your heart, however, you must be able to trust one another. Trust comes with time. As you share on a deeper and deeper level, your trust is strengthened.

RULES FOR GOOD COMMUNICATION

Good communication requires certain rules and guidelines, which are simple in one sense and extremely difficult in another.

Rule #1: There Will Be No Nonsubjects—Period

What is a nonsubject? It's a subject, for whatever reason, that is understood to be off limits and not to be brought up under any circumstance.

Several years ago, Alan had a standing weekly appointment with three other men. They covered a variety of subjects, from ministry to sports to children to wives—whatever happened to come up. When the subject turned to wives, Craig asked Joe if he and Linda ever discussed Linda's weight problem. "No way!" was Joe's response. "That is a nonsubject."

Some couples can't talk about money. Others will not discuss sexual matters of any kind. Still others won't discuss or admit past relationships. And so on. Nonsubjects between husbands and wives are not only sad but destructive. They take away from the couple's chance for intimacy—for a heart-to-heart, soul-to-soul relationship.

It takes two very mature people to handle painful subjects, but for the sake of a marriage, nonsubjects must become discussable subjects. It will take some time and understanding to get to this point. You must create a safe environment so that neither spouse feels cornered or suffocated. Patience is the key—don't give up until all subjects are open for discussion.

Rule #2: Whatever You Say, Say It with Love (Eph. 4:15)

The more difficult something is to hear, the more gently and tenderly it must be said. Honesty without gentleness is brutal. No one likes to hear negatives. That's why we must be very careful. First, make sure that what you have to say needs to be said. Is this just one of my little wishes or desires, or is it really something I need to communicate? Second, pray—ask God to give you wisdom about what to say and when to say it. Third, remember that men are really very vulnerable. Even though they may put on the macho, tough-guy exterior, they can easily be wounded.

Rule #3: Timing Is Everything

Don't try to talk about a difficult subject when the house is in chaos—the dog's barking, the phone's ringing, the kids are screaming, and so on. Make a date—go to a quiet restaurant and talk to him after he's had a good meal. Don't try to talk when he's getting ready to drift off to sleep. Your mind may be racing, but remember, he may not have picked up on your nonverbal messages and therefore has no clue you're struggling with something.

Rule #4: Get to the Point

Don't say more than you have to. Most men are bottom-line kind of guys. They don't need a lot of background information or the details about how you arrived at your dilemma. Give him the bottom line first, then go back and sketch in the details. He'll understand more of what you're saying. If he wants more information, he'll ask.

Rule #5: If He's Not Looking at You, He's Probably Not Listening

This is another good reason to talk in a restaurant. There are less distractions—for both of you. If you see his eyes drifting, it probably means you've said too much. He's lost interest. Get back to the point.

Rule #6: He Can't Read Your Mind

No matter how much your mom could read your mind, your husband can't, and he shouldn't have to. If you're not willing to say it out loud, let it go. Don't expect him to pick up your nonverbal hints. He doesn't work that way, and it's wrong for you to expect it of him.

Rule #7: Be As Positive As Possible

This attitude will earn you the right to be heard. If you talk about problems all the time, he will tune you out. If you're positive most of the time, he'll be much more willing to listen when you've got a problem (see Eph. 4:29).

Rule #8: Once You've Shared Your Concerns, Be Quiet and Listen

Don't react; just listen. Your listening will let him know you are not attacking him and you value his input. When you listen, you become partners instead of enemies. In James 1:19 we read, "Dear friends, be quick to listen, slow to speak, and slow to get angry."

Rule #9: When the Time Comes, Be Willing to Accept Correction from Your Husband

Don't be defensive. He must also be allowed to share concerns in a nonthreatening atmosphere.

Rule #10: Be Forgiving

Give your husband room to fail. Colossians 3:13 tells us to "bear with each other and forgive whatever grievances you may have against one another. Forgive as the Lord forgave you" (NIV). It's a gift you give to one another.

You and your husband may want to read and discuss the five levels of communication and the ten rules together.

The night Alan asked me to marry him, our communication was less than perfect, to say the least. I'd never dated in high school and was wary of guys to begin with. I was overwhelmed when this really handsome guy (Alan) started paying attention to me and actually seemed to like me.

The setting was the late sixties, shortly after Woodstock, and the free love movement was in full swing. In fact, a few months earlier, a guy "friend" asked me to travel around the country with him in his Volkswagen bus. I was shocked!

After several months of dating, Alan walked me to my door one night. "What would you think if I didn't have to take you home anymore?" he asked. I didn't understand the true meaning of what he said because of the experiences I'd had. I thought he was asking me to live with him, and I was horrified. I said, "I'm not that kind of girl," and started crying.

"What kind of girl? What are you talking about?" He was confused. Fortunately, he continued to ask until I was clear about his meaning. If we hadn't worked on discovering the meaning behind the words he'd spoken, that could have been the end of our relationship.

One thing I learned that night was to be careful not to jump to conclusions. I could have missed the best opportunity of my life!

Chapter 6

NO MAN IS AN "EASY KEEPER"

As a young girl, I dreamed about horses. I read horse books. I watched movies about horses. I talked about horses. I drew pictures (I tried, anyway) of horses. My love for horses was a passion.

I even got to ride horses a few times. I loved putting my foot in the stirrup, pulling myself up by the saddle horn, throwing my leg over, and sitting tall—on top of the world. I loved the feeling of power. I loved the creak of the saddle. I'd always pat the horse's neck and say, "Good boy, Apache." It was exhilarating!

Then, when I was ten, my family went on one of those guided horseback rides, and I discovered horses had personalities—they weren't like the ones you'd ride for ten cents at the grocery store. We went on one of those trails where the same horses had ridden hundreds of times. Everything was going great—I was sitting tall, pretending to know what I was doing—until we came to a small stream and my horse refused to go. I kicked the horse with my heels, but he refused to budge. He kept moving his head up and down, like he was trying to get his head free, but I refused to let go of the reins. Finally, about the time I was really starting to panic, the guide came back, whacked the horse on his rump, and we continued.

A few minutes later, I learned that all my tired horse wanted was a drink of water! I felt terrible the rest of the trip. I could picture him dying, falling to his knees, then to his side with his tongue hanging out, and it would be all my fault. I told him over and over how sorry I was.

I had a few other horse adventures, and as I look back, none of them were all that fun. Several times I had horses try to buck me off. I had a few horses unexpectedly jump over fallen logs, nearly sending me over their heads. I also had horses try to bite me, kick me, and knock me off their backs. I've come to the conclusion that I'm not a horse person after all. I guess what I really want is the fun of it without the hassles.

That's what many of us want in our marriages—the fun stuff, without the "hassles." We want the end result—an easy ride without the bumps and bruises that accompany it. When we avoid the tough stuff, we fall into one of two traps. Either we become complacent, or we go all out trying to control and change our husbands. Both traps are death to a healthy relationship. Let's take a closer look at both approaches.

COMPLACENCY

The first trap is complacency. It means we've either given up and don't want to try anymore, or we've become so comfortable or tired that we don't want to spend the energy to change the situation. Our energy is often eaten up elsewhere—children, activities, career. You name it, we're involved in it. I'm not saying any of these ways in which we expend energy are wrong in and of themselves. The problem comes when they take so much time and energy that we don't have anything left for our marriages.

I understand from some of my friends who are horse people that some horses that need very little upkeep. You can feed and water them, and they're content. They're ready when you are and willing to do whatever is asked of them without any fuss. They're just easy to get along with. This kind of horse is called an "easy keeper."

That's what many of us want in a husband—an "easy keeper."

That's what Chris thought she had in Kirk. Unfortunately, she learned the hard way that Kirk wasn't an easy keeper. Busy with many outside activities, all of them good, she assumed Kirk was doing fine. They'd spend time with each other, and he'd always been so easy-going and nondemanding, she figured everything was great. Fortunately for Chris, she realized her husband was hurting before too much damage was done.

Kirk, in fact, was tired of not having Chris's attention. He longed for the emotional intimacy they'd once enjoyed.

Chris is a rescuer. She loves to be involved in others' lives—especially those in need. It energizes her. In thinking she had an "easy keeper" husband, she lost sight of her main focus. One day, as she described several situations of families in crisis to her husband, he replied, "I'm concerned, too, but I wish you'd spend as much time working on us as you do other people."

That's what happens to many of us. We have our fingers in so many pies that we neglect the things that are most important. Children, work, and other activities demand so much of our time and energy, and we become so frazzled or exhausted that we have nothing left to give to the most important human relationship in our lives. Because we allow others to dictate how we spend our time, we have nothing left to give our husbands. We become complacent.

I have a closet in my house that needs cleaning periodically. It gathers things that don't belong there, and the things that do belong there rarely get put back. Consequently, I end up cleaning it every month or two. I wait until I *have* to clean it, which is generally when the doors no longer close. If it weren't in the hallway, I'd probably not do it so often.

An interesting thing happens when I begin to clean. First, I take almost everything out so I can organize it and put it back where it belongs. Now, if you'd come to my house when I'm in the middle of this closet cleaning, you'd wonder why I didn't just let it go. By the looks of it, you'd think I was better off leaving it alone. However, if you stick around long enough, you'd see that it's in much better shape when I'm finished with it.

What's the point? Most of us treat our marriages the same way. We ignore the closet until the doors pop open, spilling everything into the hallway. We assume that as long as the doors are closed, everything's fine.

This is complacency. It's taking our husbands for granted, assuming they're going to be there no matter what. We get comfortable in our routine. Complacency is a dangerous threat to a healthy relationship. When you run out of the "want to," it's tough to get it back.

This is where Chris found herself after twenty-seven years of marriage. She and Kirk had always had a good marriage. "On a scale of one to ten, it was about an eight," says Chris. "By the time I realized what was going on, we'd slipped down to a six.

"I made a conscious effort to turn my marriage around," says Chris. Over the next three months, Chris worked diligently at refocusing her priorities. She wanted Kirk to know he was more important to her than anything else. "It was a very painful time," Chris admits, "one I'd not like to repeat, but I'm glad it happened. My marriage has improved over what it was, and I've become more sensitive to others who are having marriage problems. I realized no man is an 'easy keeper.' Even a horse who's an easy keeper will eventually fall apart if you don't care for it."

CONTROL

The other trap we fall into is the controlling, nagging, never-satisfied attitude. This is like straightening the closet every time we walk past it. We always see something out of place and have to stop and make it right. It's like constantly fixing something that isn't broken.

Closets and husbands are two different things. The closet isn't going to feel like a failure if you clean it all day long every day. However, our husbands will feel like major failures if we constantly pick at them. What we're saying when we do this is, "I don't trust God to work in your life, so I have to."

You can see how unhealthy this kind of relationship is. Everyone is miserable in this kind of home. No one wins. In Proverbs 21:19 we read, "It is better to dwell in the wilderness, than with a contentious and angry woman" (KJV). The world beats our men down enough. We don't need to add to it.

Complacency or control. Neither one is healthy. Our goal should be to have a healthy, growing relationship where both husband and wife feel loved and supported.

Most of us appreciate 80 percent of our husbands' qualities, and don't appreciate 20 percent. I'm sure the percentage is different in some homes, but either way, our response should be the same. The key is to focus on the positive and ignore the negative. This probably sounds like an impossible task, but it can be done.

Remember the Ann Landers thirty-day experiment in chapter 2? The woman who wrote in decided not to utter one negative word to her husband for thirty days. This is a great start, but let's add one more element—saying positive things to our husbands instead. Look for specific ways to assist him, support him, and generally encourage him.

Many years ago I decided not to focus on Alan's negative qualities. I've worked hard not to let them enter into my thoughts. When he did something that irritated me, I'd think about all the positive things and not entertain anything negative. I never told him I did this. I took the Proverbs 21 verse seriously.

I haven't done it perfectly, but I think I'm more positive than negative. Just a few years ago, Alan asked me where he thought he could improve. He said, "Honey, what would you say are my weaknesses?"

It was my big chance, but after thinking about it for a while I said, "I can't think of any."

"What do you mean you can't think of any?" he asked. "I have so many."

I replied, "I don't focus on your weaknesses. What good would that do?"

By God's grace, I've chosen to focus on the positive, not the negative. It freed Alan to look to God to show him where he needs to improve rather than to me.

In Philippians 2:14 we read, "In everything you do, stay away from complaining and arguing," and in Philippians 4:8 we read, "Fix your thoughts on what is true and honorable and right. Think about things that are pure and lovely and admirable. Think about things that are excellent and worthy of praise."

If we could stop complaining and arguing, and think about positive things, our marriages would be so much better.

On many days I don't feel like being positive, and God brings a few questions to my mind. "Do I love you?" he asks. Of course, I must admit, he loves me. "How much do I love you?" he continues. Beyond imagining. I'm reminded of Ephesians 3:19: "May you experience the love of Christ, though it is so great you will never fully understand it"; and John 3:16: "For God so loved the world that he gave his only Son, so that everyone who believes in him will not perish but have eternal life." I bask in his love for a few minutes, contemplating his tremendous love for me. Then I hear him ask another question, "How much do I love your husband?" I pause. I guess I have to admit that he loves my husband as much as he loves me. Then another question, "Where do I live?" According to 1 Corinthians 3:16, he lives inside me. "Do you not know that you are the temple of God and that the Spirit of God dwells in you?" (NKJV). Then the final question, "If you don't *feel* like loving your husband, aren't you blocking my love from flowing through you?"

God loves me. God loves my husband. God lives in me. If I get out of the way, God can love my husband through me. We can take four steps to more effectively allow God to love our husbands through us.

First, discover how much God loves us through reading his Word. Second, bask in this love. In her book, *The Perfect Love,* Ruth Myers writes:

> "This is real love," we read in 1 John 4:10. "It is not
> that we loved God, but that He loves us and sent His Son
> as a sacrifice to take away our sins" (NLT). This is real
> love. This is where we find the kind of love we most
> deeply need—not in human relationships, but in God. If

we want real love, ideal love, perfect love, God's heart is
where to find it. It's the only love big enough to meet the
God-sized needs of your life and mine.[1]

Third, remind ourselves how much God loves our husbands. And
fourth, ask God to love our husbands through us—to use our mouths,
hands, and eyes to show his love to them. Chris was able to save her
marriage, but you don't need to wait until your marriage reaches a crisis point. You can begin working on these principles today, whether
your marriage is in trouble or not.

Remember Ruth and Jim from chapter 1? She was the woman
whose husband committed adultery. She followed these four steps and
God restored her marriage too.

I'd like to repeat a portion of what she said, then give you her five
principles to combat complacency and the desire to control in her marriage. "I purposed in my heart to love Jim the way I was experiencing
God's love for me. I began doing things for him out of this love. I had
no motive but to love Jim unconditionally. I was expecting nothing in
return. I didn't even know if he would stay. Over the next nine months,
I saw God love Jim through me. I was sort of a bystander, and I watched
as God drew him [Jim] into his arms of love too."

1. Appreciate your husband's hard work as a provider. "I've
   learned to thank Jim for everything he provides," Ruth
   says, "even if it's not as much as I want. I don't pressure
   him to make more, as I used to. I purpose to be content,
   no matter what happens, and that's freeing for both of us."
2. Being angry or upset doesn't have to threaten the relationship. "We've learned to be angry or upset at the situation," she says, "not each other. It takes the sting out of
   the problems."
3. Be careful to tell the truth in love. "I always ask myself if
   resolving this conflict is worth it. Some are, and some
   aren't," she says. "You have to be very discerning. Recently
   I was able to tell Jim, 'I love you, but I hate the way you

procrastinate.' He said, 'I hate the way I procrastinate too.' It opened up a very good and profitable conversation. We discovered that behind Jim's procrastination was a lot of fear of failure. We were both glad I brought it up."

4. Never nag. "It gets you nowhere," she says. "He becomes resentful, and you become frustrated."

5. Respect your husband's leadership. "I'm able to do this by putting my hope in God," Ruth states. "He [God] is my security because I know he works through my husband as the head."

Ruth learned to allow God to love her husband through her, and it changed her marriage. God performed a miracle.

Marriage is not about us. Marriage is not about our husbands. Marriage is about God.

During a seminar at our church, Dr. John Sailhammer included a note about this subject: "Marriage between two individual persons, capable of both fellowship and unity, is a picture of the kind of fellowship that man was intended to have with God. It is also a reflection, a likeness, of the kind of divine fellowship within the persons of the Godhead."

Marriage is really about God. A man and a woman are to reflect what God looks like. When a couple lives in "full-faced touch" with Christ, their marriage reflects it. It's a beautiful and intimate relationship, one that works together rather than separately. It reflects a oneness the world knows nothing of.

Joe Aldrich writes, "The number one evangelistic tool in America today is a successful marriage, because it's a living miracle."[2]

In Ephesians 5:31–32 we read, "As the Scriptures say, 'A man leaves his father and mother and is joined to his wife, and the two are united into one.' This is a great mystery, but it is an illustration of the way Christ and the church are one."

God intended for the world to see marriage and by it to be drawn to him. It's what he wants for our marriages—fellowship—intimacy—oneness.

Dr. Sailhammer also writes, "It hardly seems accidental that the Bible itself begins and ends with a marriage celebration (Gen. 2:23; Rev. 21:1–2). In Genesis 1–2, the creation of the 'heavens and earth' is followed by a marriage celebration, just as in Revelation 21:1–2 the creation of the 'new heavens and new earth' is followed by a marriage celebration. The marriage of a man and woman is the clearest example of the relationship between God and man, Christ and the church (Eph. 5)."

It doesn't just happen. We must allow God to work through us to show his love to our husbands. It's a great honor and privilege to show the world a picture of the Godhead. Many of us aren't able to show the world much more than chaos—no wonder the world doesn't want anything to do with Christianity. It's time to get the focus off us and back where it belongs—on God.

Marriage is not about us. Marriage is not about our husbands. Marriage is about God. Let's not get in the way of the message.

Chapter 7

THE GRASS
IS *NOT* GREENER

" Simon, son of John, do you love me more than these?" Jesus asked.

All our eyes were on Peter. What would he say?

"Yes, Lord," Peter replied, "you know I love you."

Good answer, Peter.

"Then feed my lambs," Jesus told him.

What? What does that have to do with love?

Jesus repeated the question: "Simon, son of John, do you love me?"

What in the world was Jesus doing? We sat perplexed, trying to figure out what he was getting at.

"Yes, Lord," Peter said, "you know I love you."

What else *could* he say?

"Then take care of my sheep," Jesus said.

This is getting weird.

Once more he asked him, "Simon, son of John, do you love me?"

We could see the hurt and shame on Peter's face as he dropped his head and said, "Lord, you know everything. You know I love you."

Jesus said, "Then feed my sheep. The truth is, when you were young, you were able to do as you liked and go wherever you wanted to. But when you are old, you will stretch out your hands, and others will direct you and take you where you don't want to go."

Whoa! I'm glad I'm not Peter. That's pretty heavy stuff.

Then Jesus told him, "Follow me."

Then Peter did the most incredible thing. I mean, Peter was always a man to speak his mind, but this was a little much even for him. I could see him as he looked around at the rest of us, his eyes landing on John. I heard Peter take a deep breath and begin.

"What about him, Lord?" he asked, pointing at John.

We all held our breath. Jesus replied, "If I want him to remain alive until I return, what is that to you? You follow me."

Pow! Right between the eyes. At first, you could see the hurt and unbelief in Peter's face, then anger, and eventually brokenness. The rest of us just watched, glad we weren't the ones rebuked by Jesus.

In the silence that followed, Jesus' eyes searched each of our faces. I tried to make myself invisible, you know, like you do in school when you don't want to be called on.

Then a cold sweat engulfed me as Jesus turned and looked at me with eyes that penetrated my soul. I wanted to run and hide. I looked down and silently pleaded, "Please don't ask me—please don't ask me." As I peeked at him from the corner of my eye, I could see he'd moved on to the next disciple. I began to relax. Just as my pulse was almost back to normal, I heard his voice.

"Theda, do you love me?" Jesus asked.

"Yes, Lord," I managed to squeak.

"Feed my sheep," he replied.

I took a deep breath. "Well, Lord, I don't mean to be rude, but what exactly do you mean by that? Are we talking literal sheep here, or do you mean something else? And how am I supposed to feed them? After all, I don't have a lot of extra money—you know that. Besides, I don't even know what sheep eat. I mean, are they meat eaters, or what? And Lord, I don't know if you've ever noticed, but they're kind of smelly, and . . . well, no one else I know has to feed your sheep. I mean, look at Mary—she has enough money she could hire someone to come in and feed them for her. Why doesn't she ever have to do it? Or maybe you could give me some extra money so I could hire someone. What do you think? What I'd really like to do for you, Lord, is be an up-front person. After all, I don't mean to brag, but I can get people to laugh. Or what about singing? You could give me a voice like Shannon or Cindy—people love it when they sing. I could really belt out those tunes. Or better yet, maybe you could make me a famous actress. I could really wow them. And I could use a *little* of the money to hire someone to feed your sheep. Or maybe . . ."

"ENOUGH!! If I want to give other people wealth or fame or beautiful singing voices, what is that to you? You follow me!!"

"Yes, Lord," I whispered.

Hebrews 13:5 reads, "Let your conduct be without covetousness; be content with such things as you have" (NKJV).

If we really stopped to think about what our discontent is really saying, we'd be very surprised and ashamed. Basically, we're telling God we don't like what he gives us; we don't really believe he has our best interest in mind; we don't think what he's given is enough. We haven't yet discovered what Paul discovered in Philippians 4:11: "I have learned to be content whatever the circumstances" (NIV).

Jackie's dad was a pastor. She was the youngest of five children. Home was a safe and loving place. "My mom and dad had a great relationship. My dad was a very loving husband. We were a close family—very affectionate. I think seeing the wonderful way my dad treated my mom contributed in part to my discontent later."

Jackie came to Christ when she was just five years old, attended Christian schools, and finished high school a year early.

Feeling stale in her relationship with the Lord, Jackie enrolled in a one-year Bible school where she enjoyed the in-depth studies. "All my life I had the misconception that God was just waiting to catch me doing something wrong. The Bible school really helped me view my relationship with the Lord from a much healthier perspective. Now I wanted everything God had for me."

She and Dave began dating when she was twenty-one. Eight months later, they were married. They got involved in a church and began attending a home Bible study as well as other church activities. Two years later their son was born. It was a difficult pregnancy, and they almost lost him. Soon afterwards, they bought a house several miles from church, family, and friends. "I felt isolated, but the house was one we could afford."

Dave was a quiet man, not very expressive physically or verbally. It was tough for Jackie, who'd grown up in a very affectionate family. She felt starved for his attention. It seemed like every time Jackie tried to bring the subject up, they would end up arguing. "I hate conflict, so I withdrew."

Their daughter was born when their son was four. Within a month, a close friend of Jackie's began a losing battle with cancer. Over the next year, Jackie spent as much time with Stacy as possible. Stephen, Stacy's husband, had been a friend of the family for twenty years. As soon as Dave would come home from work, Jackie would be out the door. Slowly, the cancer spread from one part of Stacy's body to another.

Jackie would visit Stacy in the hospital. Then she'd be off to another hospital to visit her nephew, John, who was also dying, then her dad, whose health was slowly deteriorating. "John died on Monday, and Stacy died on Saturday the same week. It was a tough time, but Stacy was such a godly woman, with an incredible testimony clear to the end."

"After Stacy died, I remember not wanting to go home. Things seemed hopeless. I'm sure Dave, in his own way, wanted to help me, but I don't think he knew what to do, so we never really talked. I felt more and more isolated all the time."

Initially, Jackie and Stephen called each other to give support and be a listening ear. "We'd always been good friends, and it was comforting to have someone to talk to about Stacy."

"Stephen and I would talk several times a week. I'd tell him about my strained relationship, and he would listen. The more Stephen and I talked, the more comfortable I was with him and the less comfortable I was with my husband, Dave. My love-starved heart soaked up the attention. Stephen made promises about the future and taking care of me. He was providing me with everything I had always dreamed of. He was attentive and involved in our conversations. I began rationalizing and convinced myself my relationship with Dave wasn't going to work out. I *wanted* it to be hopeless because I wasn't happy."

Jackie and Dave met with a counselor at their church, but it didn't seem to make any difference because she'd already made the choice in her heart. The relationship continued to deteriorate. She found a job and began working evenings. When Dave would come home from work, she'd leave.

> In my wildest dreams, I never thought adultery and divorce would ever be associated with my name. I never thought I'd be capable of making the kinds of decisions I made. I knew I had to find a way to justify being in an adulterous situation and leaving my husband without biblical cause. I convinced myself I was doing the right thing for everyone concerned—especially myself. I believed Dave was not fulfilling his biblical role to "love his wife as Christ loved the church." It's difficult to talk about the choices I made because they were so wrong. On the human level, I was "in love" and happy with Stephen.

When the relationship with Stephen turned physical, Jackie quit going to counseling, moved out of the home she shared with Dave, and filed for divorce. "The sad thing is, right about this time Dave was ready to change and do whatever it took to make the marriage work. I wasn't willing. Then my dad died. His memorial service was on the day my divorce was final."

Heartsick over the choices Jackie was making and exhausted from trying to reason with her, members of her family withdrew from her. "My mom stuck by me through all this. She made it very clear she didn't approve of what I was doing, but she also made her love and unconditional acceptance clear.

"When Stephen asked me to marry him, I told him I had to think about it. Because my family had withdrawn from me, it made me stop and think about what I was doing. It was the first time in my life I'd lost that family relationship. I needed their approval. I told Stephen I couldn't marry him. Somehow I couldn't do that to my family or my children."

Jackie renewed her relationship with the Lord over the next few months. That's when Ben came into the store she worked in, and they started talking. They'd known each other fourteen years earlier. His wife had left him for another man.

They started dating. "I didn't think anyone could ever find anything of value in me again. Ben was handsome and seemed to be a strong spiritual leader. He got me involved with working out at the gym. He talked about how he loved children. He wanted a wife who would care for his needs and cook his meals. He was charming and fun to be around. I thought he was an answer to prayer.

"Once again, I made the decision on what I thought would make me happy. I really believed *this* marriage was everything I ever wanted. I now know I should never have married him. I had no biblical liberty."

The first four months were great. "I was determined to make this marriage work. I cooked his favorite meals. I worked out with him. I really poured myself into it." Then Jackie started noticing little things. "Ben would lie about the smallest things. He would do something and blame the kids. He started making little comments about other women—how this one looked good, or how slim that one was. It was unnerving. He didn't want to spend money on me anymore. He bought a home and put it in his name only."

Jackie thought she'd done something wrong to make Ben treat her like he did. She thought counseling might help. It didn't. Ben went one time, then wouldn't go anymore.

> He's happiest if things remain on the surface. He's unwilling to open up to anyone. He doesn't want anyone to know what's going on inside. It wasn't long before there was no emotional or physical involvement.
>
> I soon realized appearance was everything to him. He can act happy when people are around. He plays with my nieces and nephews—throws them up in the air, and so

on—but when he's home, he's just the opposite. Anytime we have a disagreement, he asks me if I want to get a divorce. I feel totally defeated and trapped.

The Lord prompted me to seek forgiveness from the counselor Dave and I had been seeing before the divorce. It was an incredibly humbling experience. I wished I could have crawled in there. I think it would have felt more natural. My counselor couldn't have been more forgiving and reassuring. It was a wonderful restoration.

I've also asked Dave's forgiveness, and anytime the Lord brings to mind some new offense, I ask Dave's forgiveness again. He's been very forgiving. If it were the other way around, I'm sure I wouldn't be as forgiving.

I've asked my children's forgiveness. My daughter was too young to realize all that was going on. In fact, one day she was looking at some old pictures of Dave and me. She asked, "Why are you in this picture with my daddy?" That hurt me deeply, because I saw *my* sin affecting my children.

I'm incredibly ashamed of what I did. It was wrong. No one could condemn me more than I have already condemned myself. I wish I could undo what I've done. I wish I'd listened to my counselor, pastors, elders, and friends. I wish I could have my friends and family relationships back. I wish things could be as they were. I wish I'd been more concerned with doing what was right and more willing to be content. I've discovered discipline weighs ounces, and regrets weigh tons.

Jackie has allowed me to tell her story to convince others to "be content whatever the circumstances." After reading this chapter, she wrote to me, "Maybe God will use this to stop someone from making the same mistakes I did. Even though forgiveness is in place, it's never worth living with the burden that is the result of such choices. Tons, tons, tons ..."

Chapter 8

MY LOVER,
MY FRIEND

"'*I* am my lover's, the one he desires. Come, my love, let us go out into the fields and spend the night among the wildflowers. Let us get up early and go out to the vineyards. . . . And there I will give you my love'" (Song of Sol. 7:10–12).

This woman was excited about her husband's lovemaking! It's a picture of what God intended all of us to experience. When we don't, we don't have all God has in mind for us. Let me ask you a question. On a scale of one to ten, how would you rate your enjoyment of your sexual relationship? If we're honest, most of us would say it's not a ten. For some of us, even reading this is uncomfortable. I'd like to discuss some causes and solutions for improving our sexual relationships, especially if they're less than satisfying. But before we tackle these issues, let's take a look at what God originally intended. Let's try to set aside any preconceived ideas about sex and look at how God views it.

God has given us sex as a gift to enjoy. He wants us to experience the oneness and intimacy that a healthy and dynamic sex life provides. Genesis 2:24 reads, "Therefore a man shall leave his father and mother and be joined to his wife, and they shall become one flesh" (NKJV). Although the one-flesh relationship involves whole-person intimacy (emotional, physical, mental), the core meaning here points to the sexual union between a man and a woman (see 1 Cor. 6:16). Sex was God's idea. It's not dirty; it's holy. God's original intent was for sex to be holy and intensely enjoyable.

Did you know that our sexual intimacy is to be part of our worship of God? "Therefore, whether you eat or drink, or whatever you do, do all to the glory of God" (1 Cor. 10:31 NKJV). The "whatever" includes our sexual experiences with our husbands. Does this surprise you or make you uncomfortable? For many, this is a new concept because our ideas about sex are so twisted by society. Furthermore, because of prior inappropriate experiences with sex, it's often impossible to believe God wants to be part of it.

In his book, *A Song for Lovers,* a paraphrase of the Song of Solomon, S. Craig Glickman explains God's reaction to the couple's lovemaking. "He takes pleasure in what has taken place. He is glad they have drunk deeply of the fountain of love. Two of his own have experienced love in all the beauty and fervor and purity that he intended for them." Would you be willing to invite Jesus into your bedroom?

Unraveling our wrong ideas about sex is difficult. Our society has so perverted this part of our lives, it's almost impossible to see it the way God intended. Sex sells, so we find it misused everywhere—in grocery stores, video stores, clothing stores, television, newspapers, movies, sports, magazines, and the Internet. The list is endless. We're constantly bombarded by subtle and not-so-subtle incorrect ideas about sex. It's everywhere, and it's so distorted, it's criminal.

Take a look at chapter 5 of the Song of Solomon. Here we find a young woman who's definitely exploring her sexual feelings for her new husband. "'My lover tried to unlatch the door, and my heart thrilled within me. I jumped up to open it'" (v. 4). This is what God wants us to be—anticipating and excited. This is healthy and right.

In verses 10–16, she describes her lover in a physical way. She talks about his complexion, his head and hair, his eyes, his face, his lips, his hands, his abdomen, his legs, then back to his mouth. She was definitely interested in more than his mind!

"My lover is dark and dazzling, better than ten thousand others! His head is the finest gold, and his hair is wavy and black. His eyes are like doves beside brooks of water; they are set like jewels. His cheeks are like sweetly scented beds of spices. His lips are like perfumed lilies. His breath is like myrrh. His arms are like round bars of gold, set with chrysolite. His body is like bright ivory, aglow with sapphires. His legs are like pillars of marble set in sockets of the finest gold, strong as the cedars of Lebanon. None can rival him. His mouth is altogether sweet; he is lovely in every way. Such, O women of Jerusalem, is my lover, my friend." (Song of Sol. 5:10–16)

"My lover, my friend"—this is a beautiful illustration of the love relationship. These two were friends *and* lovers. It's important for us as husband and wife to have times when we're just friends, with no sexual overtones. It's important to find nonsexual ways of touching—hugs and kisses that don't lead to intercourse. Shoulder rubs, holding hands, arms around each other, and so on. Be creative. We need to discover ways to improve our friendship with each other. Out of the 168 hours in a week, we may spend only a handful of those hours enjoying our sexual relationship. What about the rest of the time? Use it to develop and improve friendship. In the long run, it will improve our sex life.

However, we need to be careful not to let friendship become our only focus. Many women find friendship enough for them. As much as 68 percent say they'd rather cuddle and hug than have sexual intimacy. As many as 40 percent choose never to have sex again. One man wrote to Ann Landers with this report. "After a year of marriage, my wife said, 'Let's just cuddle.' The following day I suggested we go to her favorite restaurant. When we got there, I told her we weren't going to be seated. Instead, we would just stand by the kitchen and smell the food."

You see, sex was created as a gift to the man and the woman. It is *not* a man's sport. It is a gift to be enjoyed by both husband and wife. "The husband should not deprive his wife of sexual intimacy, which is her right as a married woman, nor should the wife deprive her husband. The wife gives authority over her body to her husband, and the husband also gives authority over his body to his wife. So do not deprive each other of sexual relations" (1 Cor. 7:3–5).

When a man and woman say "I do," they're trusting each other and no one else to meet their sexual needs for the rest of their lives. They commit to loving only one person "'til death do us part." It's wonderful if both are involved in keeping this commitment, but it's extremely painful if one chooses to eliminate sex from both of their lives. It leaves the other frustrated and without hope. This is neither healthy nor right.

God could have created us to reproduce by merely brushing against one another, similar to pollination. "Oh, honey, guess what?" the wife moans as her husband comes in the front door. "I think I'm pregnant."

"Not again!" he shouts. "Can't you be more careful?"

You see, God could have created us any way he wanted. But he chose the way he did for a reason, and in so doing, gave us a beautiful and fulfilling gift—one that brings us close and gives us a bond we can have with no other human being.

In his book *Love Life for Every Married Couple,* Dr. Ed Wheat writes,

> Physical desire with its sexual expression is without doubt the most complicated aspect of love in marriage. So many potential causes of difficulty exist, and problem solving is complicated by silence, suspicion, anger, hurt, misunderstanding, fear, or guilt, which are often hiding in the shadows. The physiological mechanisms of sexual expression are intricately complex and can be shut down at any stage; yet, when hindrances are removed, they work together smoothly, without conscious effort, to transmit an experience of tremendous thrill leading to fulfillment and complete relaxation.[1]

It is possible to have the pure, exciting, and fulfilling sexual life God created for us. What's keeping us from this "tremendous thrill leading to fulfillment and complete relaxation"? We'll answer this question and others and look at several difficulties that block sexual fulfillment.

After that, we'll introduce some things to think about as we explore the issues of sexuality.

UNRESOLVED ISSUES

Unresolved issues from the past can cause a short in our sexual wires. They may include childhood sexual traumas. "Between 63 and 85 percent of women who have experienced childhood sexual abuse report some sexual difficulties in adulthood."[2] Another issue may involve premarital relations, either with our husbands or someone else. Perhaps our husband was involved with someone else before we met, and it's a "stuck" point for us. Perhaps adultery, by either one or both of us, is causing pain. If any of these is an issue, it would be good to review the section in chapter 3 about dealing with past issues and consider contacting a professional to help sort out the past and reconnect the wires that have been burned.

These issues don't go away on their own. In fact, when they're not properly addressed, they tend to loom larger as time goes on. These are highly complex issues and cannot be adequately addressed in this book, so I've included some resources for you to consider at the end of this chapter.

INADEQUATE INFORMATION

A second issue that could cause a lack of sexual fulfillment is inadequate information. When you consider the fact that the sexual relationship is the most complex element of marriage, and no one ever talks about it, it's no wonder many couples are struggling.

Christian women are often too embarrassed to discuss sex with their husbands or anyone else. This leads to frustration and anger for both husband and wife. If God wasn't too embarrassed to create it, why should we be too embarrassed to discuss it? Many couples think that if they have to discuss this delicate issue, they're failures. This isn't true. We're not failures when we discuss children or finances or careers or housing or cars or anything else. There's no reason to think we're failures when we discuss something as complex as sexuality.

Alan and I have had a number of discussions about sex. Sometimes they lasted for hours. Without meaning to, we hurt each other, and it took time to get to the bottom of the issues. The pain was almost unbearable at times, but we were determined to keep at it until we reached a solution. It's not something I'd care to repeat, but I'm grateful we were able to work through our differences and come out with greater closeness and intimacy than we ever would have experienced without the pain and hard work. That doesn't mean we never discuss our sexual relationship anymore, because we do, but we're able to resolve the issues much more quickly now.

I've also worked hard at trying to understand the male desire for intimacy, and it has proven to be a great help in our relationship. One important factor I've learned is that most men struggle with their thought life. They have images and ideas that pop into their heads at all times of the day or night. Alan was able to help me better understand the struggles he faces daily with temptation and errant thoughts.

In his book, *The Sexual Man*, Dr. Archibald Hart, tells the story of a lawyer in his early thirties. Frank gives us a rare look into the inner feelings of a committed Christian man.

> For years I have punished myself for having sexual desires, especially if I felt those desires toward someone other than my wife. I was taught that when you are married you lose all sexual feelings toward other women. I now realize how stupid this is. I have never been unfaithful to my wife, whom I love dearly, but I just don't seem to be able to stop my sexual feelings from running amuck. I don't want these feelings; they are driving me crazy.
>
> If people really knew what thoughts were going on in my head, they'd have me sent to the nearest loony farm.[3]

Dr. Hart concludes, "Frank missed the one real truth that could have set him free from guilt and confusion: Strong sexual feelings are common to all normal men. They are determined more by hormones than by evil desire."[4]

A few years ago, after both my ovaries had to be removed and I needed to take hormones, I was surprised when my sexual interest dropped off radically. During my post-surgery checkup, I asked my doctor about the problem. He suggested I add some testosterone to the estrogen I was already taking. I'd forgotten that women have testosterone as well as estrogen and progesterone.

"Women generally have about seventy nanograms/per deciliter of testosterone," he explained. "When that level drops, so does a woman's interest in sex." We decided it was worth a try. "By the way," he continued, "guess how much a man has?" Trying to guess high, I said, "Two or three hundred?" "Between seven hundred and twelve hundred nanograms! Over *ten times more*," he stated. (By the way, adding the testosterone worked great!)

Wow! No wonder men think about sex so much. We would, too, with that many hormones in our bodies. Imagine being as hungry as you've ever been in your life. In front of you sits your favorite meal, but you're not allowed to smell, look, or taste it. Think about how frustrating that would be. Now, multiply that frustration by a thousand, and we can begin to get a feel for what our men go through all the time. This is the way God made them. It's not an accident. We need to be more compassionate and understanding in light of this information.

I know that some women reading this book have a relationship that is just the opposite of what I'm describing. I've talked with women who have a much stronger desire than their husbands. This is just as frustrating, but the solution is the same—loving, honest communication; and tender, compassionate understanding and compromise. Ignoring the frustration will not make it better.

Others of you have no idea how your body works. You may not know where your clitoris is or how to have an orgasm. You may not understand much of the technical side of lovemaking. If you're not experiencing orgasm as often as you'd like, please don't hesitate to read the resources at the end of this chapter. One woman I know had never experienced orgasm in ten years of marriage. If this is your situation, excellent information is available. (I'm sure there are other resources, but it's not a subject that comes up too often.)

PHYSICAL PROBLEMS

A third cause for a less-than-satisfying sexual relationship might be physical problems. These can range from illness to hormones to pain to medications. Any of these and more can cause your desire to drop. In my case, my sexual interest hit an all-time low when I no longer had my ovaries. Fortunately for me, my problem had a simple solution.

If physical problems create an obstacle to sexual fulfillment in your marriage, a visit to your doctor is essential. Don't let your physical problems interfere with your sexual relationship. The solution might be as simple as a change of medication.

PORNOGRAPHY

A fourth issue might be pornography. Women can get addicted to pornography just as men can. Pornography comes in many forms. It can be found in novels, books, magazines, movies, pictures, the Internet, you name it. If either you or your husband is addicted, you must get help immediately. Pornography has no place in your life. It will eventually destroy your sexual intimacy and possibly your relationship. Don't take this lightly. Good Christian people can get hooked just as easily as non-Christians. Go to a counselor who can help unravel the addiction and the damage.

LACK OF SENSITIVITY

A fifth issue is a lack of sensitivity on your husband's part.

Women love to please. We're happiest when we make others happy. It's natural and healthy for us to want to please our husbands, but sometimes in our desire to please, we don't tell our husbands our own likes and dislikes.

Most men will touch their wives' bodies the way they'd like to be touched themselves, which generally involves poking, pushing, pulling, and grabbing, most of which aren't pleasant to a woman. If you don't tell your husband what you like and dislike, he won't know how to please you. If you're too embarrassed to talk about it, find a book you can read together and discuss as you go. You'll be surprised at how much you'll both be able to open up.

Remember, we're encouraged to meet our husband's sexual needs, *not* his every whim and fantasy. We are not commanded to indulge our husbands in perversions and obsessive behaviors. God intended sexual pleasures to be enjoyed by *both* husband and wife. If you're not enjoying your lovemaking, you need to communicate with your husband. If you are unsure of appropriate boundaries for sexual intimacy, consult one of the books recommended or a Christian counselor who's familiar with these issues.

SEASONS OF LIFE

The seventh cause of a less-than-satisfying sexual relationship could be the season of life you're in right now. If you have small children, you might be so exhausted that you have no interest in anything. If your children are grown and out of the house, you may have more interest than you know what to do with. Don't feel guilty if your interest isn't what it used to be. You won't be in this season of life forever.

Many women are concerned about not keeping up with the national averages. The only thing that matters is that you and your husband are satisfied. It may mean that one week you're together several times and the next not at all. Be sensitive to each other's needs. "Normal" is what's right for the two of you.

I'm sure there are many other blocks to sexual responsiveness, but those mentioned above are the most common. Let's look now at some ideas to consider as we work on making our sexual intimacy all God intended it to be.

- Work hard at not allowing boredom to set in. We often get into a pattern of making love at the same time on the same day in the same place. Even our favorite food would become distasteful if we had it for every meal. Let's be sure we add some creativity and freshness to our times together.

- Begin thinking about your husband sexually as soon as you know you'll be getting together. This gives you time to mentally prepare. It allows you to put aside the things that have occupied your mind all day, which is often the most difficult part of getting ready. We have so much on our minds that it's almost impossible to switch gears.

- Schedule sexually intimate times together. This may sound unromantic, but it doesn't have to be. In fact, scheduling lovemaking has many advantages. It gives both husband and wife a chance to switch gears and prepare. It gives us something to look forward to. We often don't realize how much time passes between times of intimacy. Scheduling can help maintain a satisfactory timing for both husband and wife.

- Buy something your husband likes to see you in. Ask him for ideas. You might be surprised. Some men go for lingerie. Others prefer work-out clothes. Still others would rather see their wives in a suit.

- Be creative. Make your bedroom romantic—soft lights, candles, a nice bedspread. It doesn't have to cost a lot, but make it romantic.

- Put a lock on your bedroom door—especially if you have children. You'll want to feel safe when you're alone.

- Stay in shape. If you're out of shape, you won't have the energy for anything, much less sexual intimacy.

- Be friends as well as lovers. Some men have a difficult time with this because they want to be lovers all the time. Women often need the friendship before they can be lovers.

- Be involved. The more involved you are with your love-making—physically and mentally—the more you'll enjoy it. I read an article listing transcripts from actual trials. In one, the lawyer asked the witness, a woman, "Are you sexually active?" Her reply, "No, I just lie there." It's OK to take part—to be involved. Don't just lie there; be a participant!

* Remember, sex is just as much a gift to us as it is to our husbands.
* It's OK to say no at times.

Tina didn't understand all that was involved in making a marriage work when she got married, especially sexually. No one talked with her about such things when she was growing up. Since her fiancé had been sexually active before they met, she didn't think there was much need to discuss it with anyone.

Neither Tina nor her husband discussed the subject of sex with the other. Tina thought she was just supposed to do whatever her husband wanted, and her husband didn't understand what it meant to really love a woman.

After seven years, both were sexually frustrated. He was frustrated because she didn't seem to enjoy their time together. She was frustrated because she felt like an object—a plaything. She had never experienced orgasm and wasn't really sure how to.

In their frustration, they finally began talking. They were able to get some counseling, which pointed them to some good books and opened up their conversation. Over the next several years, they were able to work out their differences and are now experiencing wonderful closeness and enjoyment in their sexual relationship. He has learned to treat her with dignity and honor, and she has learned to respond and enjoy their lovemaking.

If you're not where God wants you to be sexually, take time to refocus. It may be time to communicate with your husband and determine with him what your focus should be. You may need to find a competent Christian counselor to help you work through some difficult issues. Please make this a priority for the sake of your marriage. Start today. Don't put it off until you have time. The longer you wait, the more difficult it will be.

Sexual desire (stronger than all the petty differences) is what keeps bringing your husband back to *you*. It overcomes everything else that distances you from one another. That's good. Each positive encounter draws you closer together, but each rejection drives a wedge and causes your husband to withdraw from you. You must do everything in your power to become the kind of wife God intended from the beginning— the kind of wife who keeps her husband coming back to her and the kind of wife who knows her husband is her friend and her lover.

RESOURCES

Love Life for Every Married Couple by Dr. Ed Wheat (Grand Rapids, Mich.: Zondervan Publishing, 1980). This book can change your marriage. It's a great one to read together and discuss. It deals with how to fall in love again, loving your partner sexually, and barriers to sexual intimacy, among others.

Intended for Pleasure by Dr. Ed Wheat (Grand Rapids, Mich.: Fleming H. Revell, 1993). This book is more about the technical aspects of lovemaking. This would be great for couples who need more help with the actual process—including orgasm.

Before the Wedding Night by Dr. Ed Wheat (Springdale, Ark.: Bible Believers Cassettes, Inc.). This is a set of two tapes explaining how to prepare for the first night, including mentally, physically, and spiritually. These are helpful tapes even if you've been married fifty years. (Order from Scriptural Counsel, Inc., 130 Spring St., Springdale, AR 72764; 1-800-643-3477, in Arkansas: 501-751-5722.)

The Sexual Man by Archibald Hart, M.D. (Dallas, Tex.: Word Publishing, 1994). If you want to know more about how a man thinks, this is a great book. Dr. Hart has surveyed strong Christian men and gotten their feedback on how they struggle.

Intimate Issues by Linda Dillow and Lorraine Pintus (Colorado, Springs, Colo.: Waterbrook Press, 1999). This book deals with twenty-one issues concerning a woman's sexuality. It's open, honest, and quite helpful.

Chapter 9

BEFORE YOU MARRY

I attended the wedding of a friend's daughter today. It was a very nice wedding. The church was beautifully decorated; the bridesmaids were gorgeous; the groomsmen were handsome—everything was perfect. The groom looked a little nervous, but most of them do. The bride was glowing and couldn't stop smiling—she was very fun to watch. She kept turning to smile at her maid of honor as if they had some kind of special joke the rest of us didn't understand. Everything went smoothly, and soon the pastor announced the new couple to the congregation.

As I sat there watching everything unfold before me, I wondered how committed these two young people really were—how much they really understood about the years ahead. Would they be able to tough out the bad times? Were they committed enough to stay together and work through the hard stuff when there seemed to be no hope left?

As they stood there smiling, talking, and holding each other's hands, I wondered if they will be just another statistic in a few years or if they will still be together for their fiftieth anniversary. Will he bail when she puts on a few pounds? Will she reconsider when he starts to lose his hair? What if he loses his job, or she runs up the credit cards to the max? What if he starts drinking and can't stop? What if she flirts with his boss? What if they have a special-needs child? What if she "loses that loving feeling"? How will they handle the difficulties? Will their marriage become stronger with each problem, or will it weaken and end in divorce?

When a couple stands at the altar and says "I do," they don't have a clue about the difficulties they will face together. If we knew ahead of time the pain we'd endure at the hands of the one who vowed to love us forever, few of us would marry.

This chapter is for those of you who are not yet married. I'm in no way trying to discourage you, but I want you to be realistic and count the cost before you commit the rest of your life to any man.

When I was in college, I wasn't a believer, but something stuck in my mind that a friend, who was a believer, said to me. As we were walking to class one day, he told me, "God can have every part of my life, but I will choose the woman I marry."

At the time his statement seemed odd to me, and today I'm amazed at his audacity. He did marry the woman of his choosing. She was very beautiful and had a great personality, but their marriage didn't last.

Why is it so important for God to be involved in our choice of a spouse? First, he invented marriage. He alone knows how it works best. If you were planning to purchase a personal computer, wouldn't it be helpful to have the person who created it sit down and explain how it works? So, why wouldn't you want the One who instituted marriage to give you direction?

Second, God knows you better than anyone—including yourself (see Ps. 139). He knows what makes you tick. He knows how you think. He knows it all.

Third, he knows exactly what you need. It may not be what you think you need, even as a child thinks candy is what he or she needs just before dinner, but God knows what we need and when we need it.

Fourth, his ultimate goal is for your marriage to reflect his image and to be used to draw others to himself.

Fifth, you belong to him. "For you were bought at a price; therefore glorify God in you body and in your spirit, which are God's" (1 Cor. 6:20 NKJV).

Whether you already know the man you plan to marry, are looking for him, or are happily single, I challenge you to consider some things so you can make the choice God wants you to make.

Before you even think about getting married, you need to get your spiritual "act" together. The most important relationship of your life is the one you cultivate with your Creator. No person can fill the void that God himself created in you. He alone can fill it. Don't be misled into thinking you can't be fulfilled or happy without a man in your life. A bad marriage is far worse than being single.

Suppose a man does come into your life. How can you be sure he's the one God has for you? How can you divorce-proof your marriage? Unfortunately, no one can guarantee a divorce-proof marriage because sin is part of our lives. However, there are some things you can do to minimize the likelihood of divorce. These principles can take you on the path of a great marriage if you follow them but can lead to destruction if you don't.

CHOOSE THE RIGHT SPOUSE

One of the first things I'd suggest you look for is a man who's more committed to the Lord than to you. This may not sound positive at first glance, but you'll soon realize that marriage doesn't work any other way.

Marriage is created to be a supplement to our relationship with the Lord, not vice versa. When you are more in love with the Creator than each other, your earthly love becomes a thousand times better.

I find great security in knowing that Alan has a greater commitment to God than he has to me. I know that when I'm at my worst, he's still committed to me because his first loyalty is to God, and he vowed to God he would stay with me no matter what. His vow was really to God and not to me. If he's disappointed in me for any reason, he's still committed to me because of his commitment to God. I know as I get older and my face and body sag, Alan could find many women who are more attractive than I, but his faithfulness to me is centered in his faithfulness to God.

I know Alan wants to please God more than he wants to please himself or me. That's a commitment you can build a strong marriage on. I need that kind of loyalty—the kind I know won't be broken. It's not based on my performance but on God's faithfulness.

One day not too long ago, Alan and I were waiting for an elevator. As we waited, I turned to him and asked, "Do you know what I really appreciate about you?" "No, I don't think I do," was his reply. "I've never told you how much your faithfulness means to me. My dad was unfaithful to my mom, and I wasn't really sure if I could trust you. Now I know I can, and I appreciate it so much. It gives me a sense of security and peace." Alan's faithfulness to me really hinged on his vow to God.

REMAIN PURE

Another principle I'd like you to seriously consider is remaining pure and not getting involved sexually until after the wedding. I believe one of the most destructive things a couple can do before they get married is be overly involved physically. At whatever point a couple gets involved, the rest of their relationship slows down or halts altogether. This means your emotional, intellectual, and spiritual intimacy doesn't develop as it should.

I believe one reason couples get physically involved is so they don't have to deal with other issues. It's hard work to get to know someone emotionally, spiritually, and intellectually, but it's fairly simple to get to know someone physically. Many couples know each other's body better than they know the person in the body. This could be one reason for the high rate of divorce today—a few years into the marriage, they discover the real person they've been sleeping with all this time, and they don't really like that person. Statistics I've read prove the divorce rate is higher for couples who were sexually involved before marriage than for those who weren't.

A word of caution here: Many couples, in an effort to remain virgins, refrain from intercourse but engage in a variety of other sexual activities. They may be virgins technically but aren't really pure because of their other sexual activities. I suggest that touching or caressing the breasts or genitals either under or on top of clothing, with hands or any other part of the body, is not maintaining sexual purity. In God's eyes, it's just as wrong as actual intercourse.

If you're already sexually involved, you can reverse the situation by committing to stay pure from today on, then spend time getting to know one another. This will take determination and a lot of self-control, but it will be worth the health of your marriage.

If you concentrate on 100 percent commitment to God and 100 percent purity in your relationship with your man, you will have a great beginning for a solid marriage.

COMMUNICATE

Good communication is another key to a solid marriage. The rest of your life together will be determined by how well you share your thoughts and feelings. How you handle disagreements will be the single biggest factor in your communication. If you can disagree without being disagreeable, you're most of the way there.

You might want to consider several elements of good communication. Does he *really* listen to you? Do your opinions matter to him? If your opinions don't matter, you'll have little say in the relationship. Does he listen with a willingness to change his opinion? Once he hears what you think, is he willing and able to change his mind, or does he hold to his opinion no matter what? What about his temper? Does he get angry over little things? Are you able to conclude discussions with neither of you feeling degraded? Can you discuss any topic, or are there some that are off-limits?

Your answers to these questions are important. If you see areas that cause concern, don't be naive and assume they'll take care of themselves. It won't happen. You may need to find a competent counselor—a "relational coach"—to help the two of you work through these delicate areas.

CONSIDER FINANCES

Another crucial area is money. Most difficulties in the first year of marriage can be attributed to money problems. Debt is becoming more and more commonplace these days. Some things to consider: How does he handle his money? Is he in debt? Is he too free with his money, perhaps even irresponsible? Does he spend more than he makes? Is he a hard worker? Is he able to provide for you and whatever children you may have? Will you have to work to help pay the bills after children arrive? Is he too tight with his money?

Any of these areas can cause huge problems. Again, a counselor or financial planner can help you sort through the trouble spots.

CONSIDER YOUR FUTURE IN-LAWS

In-laws can be a huge problem in marriage. They can cause more damage than all your friends put together. You may want to consider: Are his parents too controlling? Are they unwilling to let go of him? How does he handle them—especially his mother? Does he have too much respect for her? Does he have too little respect?

You need to ask yourself if you love this man enough to stay with him no matter what happens. Ruth was able to love her husband in spite of his betrayal of the relationship through adultery. Kay has been able to love her husband through job difficulties, anger, and pain. Chris was able to love her husband during his midlife crisis and the pain that brought. Love is the key—the kind of love that doesn't quit.

I met Brian and Haley Sakultarawattn a few months ago. I first read their story in the local newspaper years before. I was moved beyond tears by their tender love story.

They had been high school sweethearts. After graduating, they became engaged. Not long after, Brian was in an accident. In trying to control a fire, he grabbed a can of gas, thinking it was water. He awakened three weeks later to discover he had burns over 97 percent of his body. He was blind, and infection cost him parts of each of his limbs.

What would you have done? Said good-bye and found someone who was whole? That's not what Haley did. She stayed with her man through all the surgeries and rehabilitation. Then, when he was well enough (more than a year later), she married him.

Her reason for staying? "He's still the same person. He still has his great sense of humor and his positive outlook on life. He's changed on the outside, but he's the same on the inside."

He *was* the same person. The wrapping had changed, but not the gift inside. Many of us need to ask ourselves, "Do I love the man or the package?"

Love is one of the most misused words in the English language. We say we love a song or an ice cream flavor or a pair of jeans or an old pair of slippers or someone's hair. The truth is, most of us don't really know what love is. God loved us before we were even capable of loving (John 17:24). God loved the world so much he sent his Son to die for it (John 3:16). God loves us so much there is no way to measure it (Eph. 3:18–19). God says nothing can separate us from his love (Rom. 8:35–39). That's true love.

God loves us with a passionate, never-ending, self-sacrificing kind of love. That's the kind of love we're to have for and with our husbands—the kind that will stay no matter what, the kind that is passionate and real, the kind that won't quit when things get uncomfortable. If this is the kind of love you have for one another, you're well on your way to a successful marriage.

Can you love this man the way he is right now? Many women make the mistake of thinking they'll be able to change their husbands once they're married. They can't wait to get started. It's a very naive approach. I think we've been misled by movies, books, magazines, and television. We've seen men change for the "right woman" over and over. A man who's involved with woman after woman suddenly "falls in love" and gives up everything for her. We then imagine we have that kind of power over our man. The truth is, that's pure fiction. No man is like that, and no woman has that kind of power. It's a myth. You need to be ready and willing to live with him the way he is. Otherwise, don't marry him.

Think for a minute about all the married couples you know. You probably know quite a few. Of all those couples, how many have relationships you'd like to have? How many have an open, dynamic, passionate relationship? I'd guess very few. Most people can't come up with more than four or five good examples. There just aren't that many marriages that are awesome.

How will *your* relationship be any different? Why will your marriage be awesome, when most married couples don't experience awesome marriages? It won't. Unless you're willing to face reality, your marriage could be one of the unhappy ones.

A good marriage doesn't just happen. It's something you have to work at—to cultivate with time and effort. It's much more difficult to go back and try to restructure your marriage after you've said "I do." It's much easier to begin a marriage following the principles I've outlined in this chapter than trying to clean it up later.

If you don't believe me, talk to women who are unhappy in their marriages. Ask them what they'd do differently if they could. My guess is they'll tell you that prevention is easier than cleanup; that is, trying to put things in order after the fact. It's hard to climb out of the pit once you're in it. My advice to you is: Wait for the right man—the one God has for you. In the meantime, make sure your relationship with God is where it should be.

I don't know what kind of help my friend's daughter and her husband got before their wedding today, but I pray someone had the foresight to give them tools to use as they build their relationship. I pray they won't be another statistic. I pray the same thing for your marriage.

Chapter 10

WOMAN'S BEST FRIEND

*D*o you remember as a young girl the panic you felt when you realized you had no one to sit with at lunch? Or on the school bus? Or someone to play with at recess? I think it may be just a girl thing, but I could be wrong. It seems that guys tend to congregate while girls tend to go in groups of two or three. I remember some girls planning ahead. On the bus in the morning, they'd line up someone for recess. At recess they'd line up their prospects for lunch. At lunch they'd get someone to sit by on the bus home, and so on. . . . It was always frustrating and humiliating to ask to be with someone who'd already been asked by someone else. "I'm sorry, I already promised Jeannie I'd sit by her," the girl would say. It was also humiliating to sit by someone who was definitely "uncool" or, even worse, to sit alone.

The luckiest girls had a "best friend" who would always sit by them, eat lunch with them, and spend recess with them. I had a friend like that. Her name was Margo. Wherever Margo went, there I'd be. When she signed up for choir in the third grade, so did I. She decided she was a bass, so I became a bass too. (Our music teacher just let us sing bass.) I remember the two of us getting in trouble in the fifth grade. We didn't know we were off school property when we made our fort at recess—honest.

It was a great feeling to know that we could depend on one another. Margo had a great imagination. I loved that. We would imagine things together. We created our own fantasy world—actually, she did the creating and I sort of pretended I knew what was going on.

Then the summer between seventh and eighth grade arrived. My family moved, and I had to go to a new school. But guess what? Margo's family moved, too, and we were in the same school again! At our new school, Margo moved into a higher math class. So did I. She belonged in the class; I didn't. Then we started high school. We added other friends, and then boys came into the picture. We remained friends and were involved in each other's lives, but our friendship was never quite the same as before.

When we left for separate colleges after high school, our friendship was never the same. We only see each other periodically, but I'll never forget the bond we had when we were younger.

I recently realized how important friendships are, especially as I watch our three girls going through the things I experienced. I think girls are especially in want and need of a special friendship. We spend our lives looking for that "kindred spirit," as Anne Shirley did in *Anne of Green Gables*. We need a friend with whom we can share our deepest thoughts and know the person won't laugh at us, and we feel tremendous pain when we're unable to find that friend.

I believe that many of us look to marriage to fulfill this need for friendship. We want a best friend to give ourselves to unconditionally, and we believe our husbands will be that "kindred spirit." We want that more than anything.

So we get married, assuming we've finally found our lifelong "best friend." The only trouble is, our husbands don't realize what's happened. They've probably never experienced the "best friend syndrome" the way girls do.

Over the years, I've often mentioned to Alan that he is my best friend. To me, this is the greatest honor and compliment I could give anyone. It means he has my total trust, devotion, time, energy, loyalty, and so on. To him it's just a nice thing I say. For a long time, I couldn't understand why my expression of friendship never meant much to him. Then it hit me—he didn't get it because he didn't understand the significance. I then shared with him what a best friend is all about. I could see in his face that he was starting to get it. "I never understood," he said. "Give me some time to try to grasp how much this means to you." In a few days he came back to me and said, "I think I'm beginning to get it! I think I'm beginning to understand what a precious gift you've given me by calling me your best friend, and as a result, I'm feeling more valued and loved by you than I ever have before. Thanks for considering me your best friend."

In many ways it's healthy to have our husbands fill that best friend void, but I also think there's a danger. We need to be very careful we don't allow our husbands to take the place of God in our lives.

Generally, we've come to depend on our husbands for friendship, companionship, a paycheck, closeness, intimacy, or just "being there." This dependence is healthy for the most part.

Sometimes we transfer all our needs and desires to our husbands, and we look to them to meet our every need. We want them to fill our empty hearts with love. This is wrong. No human being can fill the void in our hearts. God never intended your husband (or children or any other person) to fill that void. It's a God void, not a human void.

Imagine your needs as a bucket. Every time something happens to wound you, it's as if a hole is punched in your bucket. As a child, each time a parent or sibling said or did something cruel or unkind to you, another hole was punched in your bucket. When a classmate or teacher ridiculed you, another hole appeared. When you had to sit with the "out" crowd, you gained several holes. Anytime anyone did or said something negative to or about you, a hole was punched in your bucket.

Each of us is left with hundreds or thousands of holes in our buckets—some large, some small, some jagged, some round. The end result is, we come to marriage expecting our husbands to fill our buckets and keep them full. God never intended for our husbands to fill our buckets. It's an impossible task for anyone.

Remember Kay from chapter 5? If anyone would have the need to look to her husband to fill her bucket, it's Kay. "I went to eight different schools by the time I was in seventh grade. My dad moved a lot because of his job. My mom was shy and didn't make friends easily, but she followed my dad and never complained."

Kay became a Christian when she was eight years old but didn't really begin growing until high school. "My dad died when I was thirteen. That's when God became my daddy. He's been my friend, protected me, and given me a lot of grace. I know he's always held me in his hands and taken care of me."

Kay got involved with a campus ministry in college, which is how she met Joe. They spent time together and exchanged phone numbers. Nine months after meeting, they were married. That was nearly twenty years ago.

Joe was everything Kay wanted in a man—hard-working, tender, and a spiritual leader. He was a successful businessman, their marriage was going great, and God blessed them with several children.

It's fortunate Kay didn't depend on Joe to fill her bucket. She easily could have gotten into that trap during their first eight years because Joe was a lot of fun, and their life was fairly trouble-free.

However, soon after purchasing their dream house, Joe's business started to fail. He responded by working longer and longer hours, becoming frustrated and angry, and blaming God. He even stopped going to church.

Financially, Joe and Kay were in serious trouble, and Kay wondered if they would lose their home. She took odd jobs to help make ends meet and became a proficient thrift and garage-sale shopper.

"I realize my husband isn't perfect—far from it—but I know he's the one God gave me," Kay says. "When Joe and I got married, we decided to ban the word *divorce* from our vocabulary. We have never used the word, even in our most heated discussions. My goal is to do all I can to strengthen my marriage—to build my house, not tear it down."

Many women have lost their husbands to illness, accidents, and divorce. If they had been depending on them to fill their buckets, their entire world would have fallen apart. I think of a book I read recently by Ruth Myers. She is a great example of someone who depends on God alone to fill her bucket.

> I experienced . . . the reality that my husband couldn't meet all my needs. Dean loved me very much, but his love wasn't perfect. Sometimes he was occupied with his own needs. Sometimes he would be away for weeks at a time. Often the Spirit would bring to mind Psalm 73:25–26, reminding me again: Only one Person is your best, your perfect life partner. Only One can be with you all the time and meet your deepest needs. You may love others as much as you can, as deeply as you will, but I [God] must be your first love. . . .
>
> In 1959, we learned that Dean had cancer. He lived only nine more months.
>
> I had lost my best and primary human love. But I wasn't alone. I still had my first love; I still had my Source of deepest satisfaction. So the bottom did not fall out of my life [bucket].[1]

In Psalm 73:25–26 we read, "Whom have I in heaven but you? And earth has nothing I desire besides you. My flesh and my heart may fail, but God is the strength of my heart and my portion forever" (NIV).

What can we do to make sure God is the strength of our hearts and our portion forever? How can we allow him to patch the holes in our buckets and fill them with his living water?

The woman Jesus spoke with in John 4:7–42 was definitely someone with an empty, hole-riddled bucket. She'd been married five times and was now living with another man.

Jesus was extremely tender and sensitive to this woman. I think that's maybe what drew her to him initially. After all, she was a Samaritan—the lowest of the low. She was a "woman of ill repute"— the worst kind; and she was a woman—without rights, without resources—about on the same level as a cow. However, Jesus actually talked with her. He deliberately engaged her in meaningful conversation. Little did she know he was going to rock her world.

I would imagine that at first she tried to use her feminine charms on him. What else did she have? Then she realized, perhaps for the first time in her life, that a man was looking at her as more than just an object. He was actually interested in *her*—in her heart, in her mind, and in her life—and what she had to say. He didn't avoid her as did the *respectable* men. He didn't undress her with his eyes but was actually interested in *her*, and he ministered to her in her inner being.

In verse 10, "Jesus answered her, 'If you knew the gift of God and who it is that asks you for a drink, you would have asked him and he would have given you living water'" (NIV).

This woman was thirsty for that kind of water. She ran back to tell the rest of the town about this amazing man, Jesus.

A few chapters later, in Luke 7:38, Jesus said, "If anyone thirsts, let him come to Me and drink. He who believes in Me, as the Scripture has said, out of his heart will flow rivers of living water" (NKJV).

God himself will fix, fill, and overflow our buckets, and we'll have water to give to others. Kay looks to God to sustain her and fill her. So does Ruth Myers. You can too. God wants to be your best friend. He wants to be there in the good times and the bad. He was with his disciples when the boat began to sink in the lake, but they didn't realize what that meant (Mark 4:35–40):

> As evening came, Jesus said to his disciples, "Let's cross to the other side of the lake." He was already in the boat, so they started out, leaving the crowds behind (although other boats followed). But soon a fierce storm arose. High waves began to break into the boat until it was nearly full of water.
>
> Jesus was sleeping at the back of the boat with his head on a cushion. Frantically they woke him up, shouting, "Teacher, don't you even care that we are going to drown?"
>
> When he woke up, he rebuked the wind and said to the water, "Quiet down!" Suddenly the wind stopped, and

there was a great calm. And he asked them, "Why are you
so afraid? Do you still not have faith in me?"

The disciples knew Jesus was in the boat with them, but they were
still afraid. Why? Because of a lack of faith. They didn't really know
him. It's hard to trust someone you don't know very well.

Recently I came across this poem written by Amy Carmichael:

Thou art the Lord who slept upon the pillow,
    Thou art the Lord who soothed the furious sea,
What matter beating wind and tossing billow
    If only we are in the boat with Thee?
Hold us in quiet through the age-long minute
    While Thou art silent, and the wind is shrill:
Can the boat sink while Thou, dear Lord, art in it?
    Can the heart faint that waiteth on Thy will?[2]

Do you feel overwhelmed, like your boat is sinking? Maybe it's
half-filled with water, and you know Jesus is in there with you. It won't
sink. Nothing can happen to you that he doesn't allow. You can trust
him, but in order to do that, you must first know him. You can get to
know him by reading, studying, and memorizing his Word; by praying
and meditating on Scripture; by worshiping and spending time with
other believers. These honors and privileges are given to us as gifts.
Walking with God is a relationship to enjoy, not a regimen to maintain. No one wants you to spend time with him or her because you
have to, especially not God. He wants you to experience his love and
compassion and healing. He wants to repair your emotional bucket—
gently and tenderly, one hole at a time.

The holes in your bucket can be fixed by trusting God with everything—your hurts, fears, past, and future. He wants to fill your bucket
with his living water—the kind that never runs out, the kind that over-
flows and runs onto the people around you.

Are you familiar with the words to "Spirit Song"? They express exactly what I'm trying to say, so I'll quote it here for you.

O let the Son of God enfold you
      With His Spirit and His love,
Let Him fill your heart and satisfy your soul.
      O let Him have the things that hold you,
And His Spirit like a dove,
      Will descend upon your life and make you whole.
Jesus, O Jesus, come and fill your lambs.
      Jesus, O Jesus, come and fill your lambs.
O come and sing this song with gladness,
      As your hearts are filled with joy.
O lift your hands in sweet surrender to His Name.
      O give Him all your tears and sadness,
Give Him all your years of pain,
      And you'll enter into life in Jesus' name.[3]

He wants you to trust him. He wants to be your best friend. "Never will I leave you; never will I forsake you" (Heb. 13:5 NIV). You never have to be alone again. You don't have to depend only on your husband or children or friends or job or anything. Jesus will be all of those and more if you let him.

Chapter 11

THE ULTIMATE
LOVE RELATIONSHIP

*H*e was the greatest, most powerful king who ever lived. He was good to his people, kind and generous. They loved him and he loved them.

She was a commoner, the lowest of the low. The other commoners had nothing to do with her. She was a mess—filthy clothes, matted hair, unkempt in every way. She got money for food any way she could. She'd lie, cheat, or steal in order to sustain her miserable life. No one paid attention to her as she huddled in her corner with only her threadbare clothes to shelter her.

In order to show his love for his people, the king decided to adopt a child from among the common people. Many children were brought to him. They dazzled him with their impeccable manners and proper speech. He applauded their extraordinary talents. He was amazed at their devotion and desire to be his child. There was nothing wrong with any of them. In fact, they were all wonderful, but for some reason, they just weren't right for him.

She never looked anyone in the eye. She couldn't stand the rejection from one more person. Orphaned as a young child, she'd been making her own way most of her life. She wasn't allowed anywhere but the street, and even there, she was hurried along by an angry merchant or housewife with a broom. Today was like any other day. She scrounged through the garbage piles, hoping she could find something before she was discovered and shooed away, as if she were nothing but a pesky fly. She no longer dreamed of a better life. Her only concern was getting enough food to sustain her for the day.

Today the king decided to look for his child himself. It was highly unusual for the king to go among the people, not that he was above that, but because he never had the time. His days were filled with requests from his people. Lines formed early in the morning and didn't let up until after dark. He loved his people, and he never tired of them, but today was different. Today he would find his child and bring her home.

Filled with eager anticipation as he dreamed of bringing his child home this very day, he rose early and dressed in his finest clothing. He was certain he'd find her.

He searched everywhere—orphanages, businesses, homes—but by noon, he had not yet found her. He stopped for lunch. "Sire, surely you must be ready to go home by now," his aide suggested.

The king sighed. "No, I know she's here somewhere. I must keep looking." By evening the king and all his officials were discouraged.

"Sire," his aide questioned, "shouldn't we go home for the night? We can start early again tomorrow."

"I must find her," the king answered.

She was tired and hungry. She hadn't been able to find anything more than a few crumbs all day. She was more tired and hungry than she'd ever been. She just wanted to lie down, but every time she stopped, someone saw her and sent her on her way. Too tired to even think, she walked with her head down, willing her body to put one foot in front of the other on the cold, hard road.

He stood tall, confident he would find her. There in the distance he saw a small, lone figure walking in his direction, her head down. As they drew closer, he saw the thick, matted hair; the filthy, ragged clothes; and the dirty, grimy body of a young girl.

He gasped, "That's her."

"Who, sire?" his aide asked.

"My daughter!" the king exclaimed as he began to run toward her.

The girl soon found herself surrounded by a group of men. She sank back, frightened.

"Don't be afraid, child," said a voice as soothing as any she'd ever heard. The last thing she felt before collapsing was a sense of security—as if she were finally home.

She was awakened by the sound of someone singing. As she opened her eyes, she saw a woman dressed in the whitest clothes she'd ever seen. "Am I in heaven?" she asked.

The sound of the woman's laugh was like the babbling brook she'd often gone to for water. "No, child, but you *are* in the king's palace," the woman in white replied as she placed a small portion of food and water before her. "The king said to give you several small meals until we get your stomach used to food again."

"Why am I here?" the child asked.

"Well, the king wants to adopt you. He wants you to be his daughter. Isn't that the most amazing and wonderful thing you've ever heard?" the woman asked. "Now, hurry and eat so we can get those filthy clothes off you and get you bathed and ready to see your new father."

"Why does he want *me?*" the child again asked.

"I don't know. He knew he wanted you from the moment he laid eyes on you. That's all I know," the kind woman said.

After the meal and bath, she dressed in the most magnificent clothes she'd ever seen. She couldn't believe the girl in the mirror was really her. It was almost as if the reflection she saw was of someone else—someone she didn't even know.

As she followed the guard in the dazzling purple uniform down the long, winding staircase, she took in all the beauty of the palace. In some ways, it felt as if she'd lived here forever. In others, she felt totally out of place, as if she were living someone else's life.

"Come in, child. I've been waiting for you," the king said as she entered the room. "Come sit here," he said as he pointed to a chair next to him. The fire in the fireplace felt wonderful and warm on her freshly washed skin. She sank into the chair the king offered.

"What is your name, child?" he asked.

"Katrina," she replied.

"What a lovely name. In fact, it's the loveliest name I've ever heard," he said. "You know, I want you to be my child, don't you, Katrina?"

"Yes, sire," was all she could manage to say.

"Well, what do you say?" he asked.

"You mean I have a choice?" she questioned.

"Of course you have a choice. It's your life too," he replied.

"What do I have to do? I mean, what are you expecting?" she asked with her eyes to the ground.

His touch was soft and tender as he lifted her chin and looked in her eyes. "Nothing, Katrina. Nothing is expected of you. I just want you as my child. I want to be your father. I want to protect you. I love you." She could see the tears forming in his eyes.

"I don't know. I'm not sure I could be your daughter. I mean, I don't know anything but the streets. How could I possibly live here? There's so much I need to learn and do," she began.

"You don't have to do anything but be my daughter," he replied.

"Could I think about it?" she asked.

"Of course," he said. "Take as much time as you need."

They spent the rest of the day wandering the castle and magnificent grounds. Each day they'd walk and talk, getting to know one another. And so it went for several weeks. Then one day, as they were walking in the garden holding hands and talking, she looked into the king's eyes and said, "I think I'm ready to be your daughter."

He picked her up and twirled her around and around until she couldn't breathe. "You've made me the happiest man to ever walk this earth," he whispered in her ear.

"I don't deserve you," she replied.

Soon the king had everyone in his kingdom scurrying around to prepare the grandest ceremony the kingdom had ever known. Every man, woman, and child was busy from sunup to sundown. Once the preparation was over, the celebration lasted a week. The whole kingdom was invited, and everyone welcomed the king's new daughter with open arms.

The king was delighted with his new daughter, and Katrina was overwhelmed at the love of her new father. He was never too busy to see her. Even the tiniest trouble was never too small to bring to him. Everyone in the palace knew when Katrina was in the room; the king only had eyes and ears for her. She would sit on his lap, and they would talk and laugh as if the rest of the world didn't exist. They were both so happy they'd found each other.

Then one morning, several months later, Katrina dressed herself in the old rags she'd worn that first day and headed for the streets. She began scavenging for food. Just about the time she was getting really hungry, she saw the king approaching.

He ran to her and embraced her as she cowered in the shadows. "I'm so glad I found you. I've been looking for you all day long," he said through his tears. "Why are you out here living like a pauper again? Don't you like the palace and clothes and food?"

"Oh, yes!" she replied. "They're all wonderful!"

"I don't understand," was his puzzled reply.

"I don't really deserve all you've given me," she said. "I don't belong there. I have nothing to give you."

"All I want is your love," he whispered. "That's all I've ever wanted. I don't want anything but you. It's the one thing I don't have. Please come home."

"Do you really want me?" she asked.

"I'd rather die than live without you," he whispered.

"You love me that much?" she gasped.

"Yes, Katrina, I love you that much," was his tender response.

"Then let's go home . . . Daddy!" she replied as she threw her arms around him.

This is a picture of God's love for us. We are that pauper girl with nothing to give and everything to receive. God, in his infinite, amazing, and unconditional love, has chosen each of us to be his adopted daughters. That's the hard part. If there was just something we could do to earn his love, it would be so much easier to receive it.

In Romans 5:6 and 8 we read, "When we were utterly helpless, Christ came at just the right time and died for us sinners. . . . But God showed his great love for us by sending Christ to die for us while we were still sinners." While we had nothing but filthy rags, God found us and brought us into his eternal family. He removed all the filth from our lives and gave us the righteousness of Christ.

What can we do to get this righteousness? Agree that we need it and that he's the only One who can give it to us.

God's love is really all we need. He's the only One who can truly meet our hearts' deepest needs. He created us with a void in our hearts, and he's the only One who can fill that need. Our husbands can't fill that void and neither can any other human being.

Human beings let us down. They can't help it. But the King of the universe will never let us down.

God pursues us. He looks until he finds us, then he invites us to come home with him and be his adopted daughters.

When I came to Christ, I felt much like the girl in the story. I was living my life the best I could. Sometimes it was tough. Even though I was surrounded by friends, I still felt lonely and sad. I was in college at the time, with no goals or specific direction. Friends would ask what I was going to do with my life. I hadn't even chosen a major and certainly had no clue about the rest of my life.

I thought that if I could just participate in some exciting event or meet the right person, I'd be happy. I spent half my time looking forward to events, and the other half depressed because they never seemed to measure up to my expectations. I was looking to people to fill the void I had in my heart.

As I look back now, I can clearly see God's hand in drawing me, even before I knew him. The choir I was part of was full of believers, including the director (amazing for a secular college). We prayed before each concert. Many of the songs we sang spoke of God's love. Then one night, March 25, 1971, before one of our concerts, a friend asked me if I wanted to receive Christ. I wasn't sure what that meant, but it sounded religious, so I agreed. As I prayed, I felt a peace come over me like I'd never before experienced. It was as if I'd found the missing pieces of my heart.

God picked me up out of the gutter and gave me something to live for. He clothed me in his righteousness. He drew me into his embrace. He threw a party in my honor.

In the mid-sixties, color televisions began to make their way into American homes. Until then, black and white was the only choice. I remember one evening at dinner, my sisters and brother and I decided to protest the fact that we didn't own a color television. We knew we were missing out on something wonderful, and we also knew Dad held all the power in this decision. We thought maybe we could influence him.

Each of us made a sign and hung it around our necks. One of the signs read, "Hey, Simon Legree, how about a color television?" (Ingenious, weren't we?) We determined we wouldn't say a word but just eat our dinner in silence with these signs on our necks. Somehow we even talked our mom into wearing a sign too. That made seven against one, so we knew the odds were in our favor. Believe it or not, we had a color television within the next month. (My dad was a soft touch.)

I remember sitting and watching that first show on our new color television with my family. We were all so excited. Not all the shows were in color, but those that were amazed us!

That's how I felt on March 25 the night my heart was healed. Nothing looked the same as it had before. It was as if everything went from black and white to color.

I wish I could say I've walked closely with my heavenly Father since that night, but it wouldn't be true. Like Katrina, I've gone back to my old ways from time to time. Still, my Father searches for me and lovingly draws me back into his embrace.

After so many years of knowing him, I'm finally beginning to believe he's all I need. And there are even times when he's all I want.

How about you? Have you ever been embraced by your heavenly Father? He's waiting to throw a party in your honor, too, you know. (See the epilogue for instructions on how to become his forever child.)

If you've made that commitment in the past but aren't experiencing his embrace, now's the time to come home—to walk with him and talk with him, to sit in his lap and call him "Daddy." Don't hang out in the streets any longer.

"Then Jesus said, 'Come to me, all of you who are weary and carry heavy burdens, and I will give you rest. Take my yoke upon you. Let me teach you, because I am humble and gentle, and you will find rest for your soul. For my yoke fits perfectly, and the burden I give you is light'" (Matt. 11:28–30).

Sometimes our burdens are so big and life is so complicated we need to step back and get a fresh perspective. A two-year-old has a very limited view of life. She sees life in terms of what's in front of her at the moment—toys, people, pets, whatever. For her, what's happening right now is life.

A ten-year-old sees life from a bigger perspective. Her world is more than what's immediately in front of her. She realizes she needs to plan for the future, so she invites several girls to her birthday party so they'll invite her to theirs. Her perspective is bigger than a two-year-old's, but not as big as someone who's twenty. (Notice, I left out teenagers—they revert to the two-year-old stage.)

A woman with small children suddenly sees life differently, often appreciating the things her mother went through. The older we get, the bigger and broader our perspective. Life starts to make sense. Because of things we've learned from the past, our decisions tend to be more careful and wiser. A two-year-old who's afraid of strangers becomes a successful salesperson at forty. Why? Because she's learned not to be afraid of strangers. Her perspective has changed.

Wouldn't it be great if we could see life from God's perspective? He sees things from a totally different vantage point than we do. Things that don't make sense to us make perfect sense to him. The great thing is, he's written down his perspective for us. All we need to do is read it.

George Mueller wrote: "I saw more clearly than ever, that the first great and primary business to which I ought to attend every day was, to have my soul happy in the Lord. The first thing to be concerned about was not, how much I might serve the Lord, how I might glorify the Lord; but how I might get my soul into a happy state, and how my inner man may be nourished. . . . I saw that the most important thing I had to do was to give myself to the reading of the Word of God and to meditation on it."[1]

Spending time reading our Bibles isn't a "nice thing" to do or even the "right thing" to do. It is the very lifeblood for our deepening relationship with the Father. Our goal shouldn't be to read the Bible. It must be God himself. He's our goal—to know him, to worship and adore him, and to live in his presence now and for all eternity. Only that kind of relationship can give us the perspective we need to live here on earth. There's no way we can make sense of anything any other way. We can't have a God-sized view of life if we don't spend time with him, allowing him to show us what he's like. Life without him doesn't make sense. With him, it does.

In Romans 8:28 we read, "And we know that God causes everything to work together for the good of those who love God and are called according to his purpose for them."

Each one of us has a specific purpose for being here on earth. It may be to show love to a husband who knows nothing about love. It may be to show those around us what a godly marriage is about. It may be to bring glory to God in the midst of physical pain. Whatever the reason, he loves us unconditionally and gives us what we need to live each day.

When two people spend lots of time together, they become more like one another. As we spend time with God, he doesn't become like us—he's perfect—but we become more like him. As we become more like him, our perspective becomes bigger and broader. The "stuff" of life has different value. Chaos is no longer chaos but takes on new meaning. Irritations become opportunities. Life makes sense.

Don't you want to come home? Aren't you tired? Can you hear him calling you? He's whispering, "I love you. Please come home. I'd rather die than live without you."

Chapter 12

ONLY ONE THING

*M*artha didn't have a clue. "As Jesus and the disciples continued on their way to Jerusalem, they came to a village where a woman named Martha welcomed them into her home. Her sister, Mary, sat at the Lord's feet, listening to what he taught. But Martha was worrying over the big dinner she was preparing" (Luke 10:38–40a).

Martha was trying to do the right thing. She just didn't know what the right thing was. She had a house full of people who needed to eat. She had the meal planned and underway but was overwhelmed at the task. I imagine that the more she worried, the angrier she got. Why? Because her sister Mary was doing nothing to help. It wasn't fair! Finally she couldn't take it any longer.

"She came to Jesus and said, 'Lord, doesn't it seem unfair to you that my sister just sits here while I do all the work? Tell her to come and help me'" (Luke 10:40b).

You have to admit, the woman had guts. She had all this work to do and all these people to feed, and she had to do it all by herself! Can't you just feel her frustration? I can.

Have you ever noticed that Jesus never gives the answer you expect? I'm struck again and again by how "other-worldly" his answers are. His answer to Martha is no exception.

"But the Lord said to her, 'My dear Martha, you are so upset over all these details! [ouch!] There is really only one thing worth being concerned about. Mary has discovered it—and I won't take it away from her'" (Luke 10:41–42).

That's it? If I'd been Martha, I'd have walked away scratching my head, confused and more frustrated than before. After a day or two or fifty, I might have put two and two together.

"There is really only one thing worth being concerned about. Mary has discovered it . . . ."

What had Mary discovered? Martha was clueless.

"Her sister, Mary, sat at the Lord's feet, listening to what he taught" (Luke 10:39).

That's the one thing—listening, listening to Jesus. Listening to what he says about life, about love, about God. That's the one thing Mary was concerned about. Martha was concerned about everything but that one thing.

What about you? Is life so busy with "stuff" that you don't have time for the one truly important thing—sitting at the Lord's feet, listening to what he has to say?

I understand. My life is busy too. But guess what? That's no excuse. If you're too busy to pray and read God's Word, something needs to change. It won't be easy. In fact, it may be one of the most difficult things you've ever done. But you don't want to miss what Martha missed—the one truly important thing in life.

As a young man, Ron Frost was challenged to read through his Bible by a man who had been doing it two or three times a year for more than fifty years. Ron was impressed with this man's knowledge of the Word and his relationship with the Lord. He says, "Sam's Bible knowledge amazed me. His Scripture awareness had penetrated all aspects of his life, not in a rote fashion, but in a way that seemed accessible and functional."[1]

Ron began reading his Bible and finished it in two months. He says, "I was in awe of God's greatness, holiness, and redemptive love. I recognized the vast and singular strength of his personality projecting through the broad range of writers and books of the two testaments. It was as if I had truly felt the beginnings of knowing God intimately."[2]

I was challenged by Ron and began to read the entire Bible. I now read through the New Testament twice every six months and the Old Testament once. It has become the highlight of my day. I'm learning so much about God and what he's like. The more I read, the more I'm in awe of him.

Ron wrote a book about this subject. I highly recommend it. It's called *Discover the Power of the Bible—How God's Word Can Change Your Life,* by R. N. Frost. You won't be disappointed. It will change your life.

Listening to God's Word is truly sitting at the feet of Jesus. God is the lover of your soul. He wants to have an intimate, vital, loving, on-going relationship with you. He sent you a love letter. It's waiting for you. Will you read what he has said to you? Will you pick it up, expecting to learn what he's like? Will you cultivate a relationship with him? It's not a duty—something that has to be checked off the day's "to do" list.

The things of this world have blinded us to the most important and fulfilling thing there is—to sit at his feet listening. That's what makes life worth living. That's what gives perspective. That's what will make a difference in your life and in my life.

My great Aunt Pauline (my dad's aunt) made the single most important contribution in my life. She never married. She never accumulated much wealth. She never traveled to exotic places. She lived all her life in North Dakota. In fact, she was an ordinary woman. I only met her once, and that was just a few years before she went to be with the Lord. In fact, I don't really remember ever talking to her, other than that one time, but she had a huge impact on me. How? She prayed. She literally prayed me into the kingdom. God used this simple woman to bring hundreds of other people to himself also.

Prayer is our most powerful tool, yet most of us rarely use it. When we do, it's mostly to ask for something or to help us get out of trouble.

In *A Treasury of Prayer,* E. M. Bounds writes, "Few Christians have anything but a vague idea of the power of prayer; fewer still have any experience of that power."[3]

Why is prayer so important? E. M. Bounds continues, "Prayer honors God. It dishonors self. It is man's plea of weakness, ignorance, want. A plea which heaven cannot disregard. God delights to have us pray."[4]

Jesus did a lot of praying. He was constantly going off by himself to pray—often through the night. He needed guidance. He needed fellowship. He needed strength. He needed his daddy. What do we need? Guidance. Fellowship. Strength. Our daddy.

Without prayer, nothing will change. With prayer, everything can change, and what will change most is the one who prays—the one who in utter dependence throws herself on the mercy of God. The one who seeks not her own but the will of the Father.

What is the purpose of prayer? I believe that in Matthew 6:9–13 (also known as the Lord's Prayer), we find the purpose of prayer, which is, to make us more kingdom-minded. Jesus is showing us that life here on earth is really about life after we die.

Our Father in heaven,
    may your name be honored.
May your kingdom come soon.
May your will be done here on earth,
    just as it is in heaven.
Give us our food for today,
and forgive us our sins,
    just as we have forgiven those who have sinned against us.
And don't let us yield to temptation,
    but deliver us from the evil one.

The whole point of this prayer is to get our eyes off ourselves and onto the bigger picture. That's what prayer is supposed to do. It causes us to see things from a whole different perspective—a heavenly, holy one. When we have the right perspective and are more interested in the things of God than the things of this earth, we see miracles!

It makes me sad to read books on prayer that discuss how God worked in miraculous ways as if he's some genie in a bottle. I've noticed that most of these prayers have to do with houses or finances or some creature comfort. I'm not saying it's wrong to ask God for those things, but it's interesting to me that you don't hear so much about people asking to be humbled or to release Christian prisoners around the world or for more money to relieve famine in third-world countries.

Selfish prayers aren't God-honoring. Selfish prayers are self-honoring.

Pray for character to be built in yourself and others. Pray for God to give you someone with whom to build a relationship so you can eventually share the gospel. Pray for the leaders of your church, that God will protect them. Pray for their marriages. Let your prayers be other-worldly so God can change your perspective and help you to see this life as only a stepping-stone to the next.

Even more important, pray for your husband. There is nothing more important that you can do for him. It will also give you an eternity-minded view. The "stuff" of life won't be as pressing and worrisome.

Colossians 1 gives great ideas for things to pray for. Starting in verse 9, we read, "We ask God to give you a complete understanding of what he wants to do in your lives, and we ask him to make you wise with spiritual wisdom."

As wives, it's extremely important to constantly bring our husbands to the Father's throne. If we don't do it, who will? To use this verse as a prayer for your husband, ask God to give him complete wisdom, to know what God wants to do in your man's life, and to make him wise with spiritual wisdom. That would be pretty awesome!

Then you can move to verses 11 and 12: "We also pray that you will be strengthened with his glorious power so that you will have all the patience and endurance you need. [Who doesn't need patience and endurance?] May you be filled with joy, always thanking the Father, who has enabled you to share the inheritance that belongs to God's holy people, who live in the light."

You could spend a long time using these three verses in prayer for your husband, but there are many more.

Remember what Jesus said? "'There is really only one thing worth being concerned about. Mary has discovered it—and I won't take it away from her'" (Luke 10:42).

That's a simple way to live. All of life can be boiled down to one thing—sitting at Jesus' feet. It will change everything. The woman referred to in the following letter discovered it. Will you?

I'd like to tell you about my daughter. She's incredible. She's withstood pressures most of you know nothing about. She married a man who said he was a Christian, but after five years of marriage, she realized that either he'd been lying or was terribly deceived.

He started drinking, then gambling, then chasing other women. My daughter came to me almost every day to ask what she should do. I told her to read her Bible every day for answers and to get involved in a good church. I said she could come to me any time she needed. I promised her it would get better someday.

She began reading her Bible, looking for passages that would explain what to do. She and I talked daily. She depended on me. I was her life support.

She found verses and shared them with me. Proverbs 31 taught her about being an excellent wife and having the heart of her husband trust in her. She became an excellent wife.

Genesis 2:22–23 taught her about being a helpmate suitable. She became a helpmate incredible!

Ephesians 5 showed her how to be submissive. She gave her whole heart to it.

Whatever she read, she applied. Then she waited. And she waited. And she waited.

She waited ten years. She waited twenty years. She waited thirty years.

Then one day, he began to change. He started reading his Bible and going to church with her. He talked with me every day too. He told me he was changing because of the attitude and love of his wife. Without her, he never would have been able to put his life back together. We all rejoiced together.

They had several happy years together after that. Then he got sick and died. He'd changed so much over the last few years they had together. Even more remarkable, however, she became the most beautiful woman I've ever seen. She glowed with the love from her heavenly Father. She lit up a room with her beauty—the beauty of a heart full of God.

She never would have been like that if it hadn't been for her husband. So you see, what may seem like a curse to you, was really a blessing. She came to live with me last year. We had a wonderful party. She received a welcome like few others. The angels danced and sang. Her husband gave her a huge hug, but most of all, she got a long embrace from me. I was so proud of her. She lived well, but most of all, she finished well. I told her, "Well done. I'm so proud of you."

Love, Jesus

Epilogue

THE MOST IMPORTANT PART

I could use some good news for a change, how about you? Well, I have some good news that could literally rock your world. Interested?

I'm living proof of its authenticity. If it weren't for the good news I heard when I was a twenty-year-old college student, I'm convinced I would have ended my life shortly thereafter.

I'm not going to sugarcoat this and tell you life is always wonderful. It's not. That's a kind of mental game some people play. I'm not into games, especially when it comes to life and death.

The bottom line is, life only makes sense when we live it according to the Master's plan. That probably seems simplistic, but it's the truth. If you knew beyond the shadow of a doubt that God had a specific plan for your life, wouldn't you want to know what it was?

Many people don't want someone else running their lives, not even God. If that's you, don't bother reading any more. This good news isn't for you. However, if you truly want to make some meaning of your life, please continue.

You don't believe in God? Do me a favor. Go outside on a clear night and look up at the stars. Where did they come from? An accident? I don't think so. Or take a trip to the ocean. Where did the beauty come from? How did it get here? Now look at your hand. I mean really look at it. Do you see the lines? Your fingerprints? The blood vessels? Don't tell me you believe you just "happened." I don't buy it, and any thinking human being knows deep down he or she isn't some accident of nature.

God is there whether you believe it or not, and he desperately wants to be a part of your life. It's hard to imagine that God would be desperate about anything, but it's true. More than anything, he wants you to know him. He loves you with a passion no human can understand. Don't ask me why because I don't know the answer. If I were God, I certainly wouldn't care about a bunch of people who care only for themselves. I'd have lost patience about two seconds after Eve took a bite of the forbidden fruit.

So now, where are we? Let's assume God is real, and he is very interested in your life and he created you for a specific reason.

If that's true, where does that leave us? I'd be very interested in finding out exactly what God had in mind when he put me together. How about you? That means he knew exactly what I would look like, the family I'd grow up in, and the man I'd marry. He'd have tailor-made them just for me with a specific purpose in mind. That would make sense of life, don't you think?

Assuming all this is true, you ask, how do I figure out what he has planned for me? The answer is so simple it's profound. You see, he came to earth to tell us about his plan in person. Is that even possible? Not for us, but it was for God. Think about it. If he's God, is anything out of his ability?

Listen to what Jesus said: "My purpose is to give life in all its fullness" (John 10:10). That's quite a purpose, isn't it? That's why he came to earth.

You know what else? He lived his entire life without sinning. You mean he never cursed or was jealous or even saw an X-rated movie? That's right.

Then guess what he did? Go ahead and guess. Oh, all right, I'll tell you. He died. So, doesn't everyone die? Well, yes, but this was a little different. But then, Jesus was different. What would you expect from someone who'd spent all but thirty-three years in heaven? He had a bit of a different slant on things. He didn't see things the way normal, sinful people see them. Actually, I'm glad he didn't. Then he wouldn't have come up with this incredible plan for you and me. You see, he died, and then three days later he came back to life. Only God could pull that off, don't you think?

Now, here's the good news part. When he died, he paid for your sin and mine. You heard right. Because he lived a life without sin, he was able to sacrifice himself to pay for our sin. We aren't sinless, so we can't pay for it ourselves.

Imagine someone loving you so much that he is willing to give up his life for you! Jesus did. He really and truly did. This isn't a fairy tale. It's the greatest reality, the greatest truth. "Christ also suffered when he died for our sins once for all time. He never sinned, but he died for sinners that he might bring us safely home to God" (1 Pet. 3:18).

So, what do you say now? Would you be willing to put your life into the hands of someone like that? Someone who would die for you? Someone who loved you that much? I hope your answer is yes. If not, please check it out. Don't close your mind to what is the most important decision of your life.

After all, if his love has made such a dramatic difference in my life— and millions of others too—couldn't he do the same for you? This is all true. I was so unhappy. I wanted to be happy. I wanted to be loved. I wanted life to make sense, but all I had was pain. That's when God reached out to me. I discovered he loved me more than any human being ever could. I felt his love. He healed my pain. He gave me a new life, and I discovered he really did have my life planned. I still don't know all he has planned, but I trust him. He's given me so much, I'm willing to go wherever and do whatever he wants. He's given me peace and love and true happiness, the kind that goes deep and stays deep.

I know he can do the same for you. I've seen it in others. I've experienced it for myself. And the Bible talks about it too.

So, let's say you're convinced. Now what? All you have to do is tell God you want to live according to his plan. Ask him to pay for your specific sins with the death of Jesus. Tell him you really want the love he has to offer. Tell him you're ready to do whatever he asks. Then thank him. It's that simple. You don't need any special tools. You don't need to get your life in order first. Just talk to him. Believe me, he's waiting to hear from you.

Guess what happens next? I know this is going to sound weird, but remember we're dealing with God here. Anything's possible, right? God himself will come to live inside of you, in the form of the Holy Spirit. That's right—inside you. Look at this: "Don't you realize that all of you together are the temple of God and that the Spirit of God lives in you?" (1 Cor. 3:16). He gives you a makeover from the inside out. Incredible, isn't it?

I remember very clearly the night I asked God to heal me. I felt whole, like something (or Someone) filled up the empty spaces. I didn't feel hopeless anymore. He healed my heart. Wouldn't you like to have the God of the universe heal you?

I hate rules, don't you? That's what some people think the Christian life is, but they're wrong. The Christian life is about God loving you and living inside you, making you whole and giving you purpose. It's a transforming love.

Oh yes, one more thing. At the end of your life—when you die—you don't really die. The Bible tells us we relocate. We leave our bodies, and the real us goes to a new home. We either enter eternity in heaven with God and experience constant pleasure or we relocate to hell—away from God—with constant torment. The second you pass away, you enter into one or the other. This is the reality of life after death. It's also not multiple choice. Heaven or hell. No other options.

Now, it's your turn. What are you going to do with this information? It would be easy to read it, put it aside, and never think about it again. I did that for a number of years. I wish I hadn't. Please don't wait. Give it some serious thought right now. It's the most important decision of your life.

NOTES

Chapter 2

1. Neil Andersen, *The Bondage Breaker* (Eugene, Ore.: Harvest House, 1990).

2. Quoted in Elisabeth Elliot, *Gateway to Joy* (Ann Arbor, Mich.: Servant Publications, 1998), 121.

Chapter 3

1. Elisabeth Elliot, *Let Me Be a Woman* (Wheaton, Ill.: Tyndale House Publishers, 1976), 22.

Chapter 4

1. Ruth Myers, *The Perfect Love* (Colorado Springs, Colo.: Waterbrook Press, 1998), 133.

Chapter 5

1. Dennis Rainey, *Staying Close* (Waco, Tex.: Word Publishing, 1989).

Chapter 6

1. Ruth Myers, *The Perfect Love* (Colorado Springs, Colo.: Waterbrook Press, 1998).

2. Joe Aldrich, *Lifestyle Evangelism* (Portland, Ore.: Multnomah Press, 1981).

Chapter 8

1. Dr. Ed Wheat, *Love Life for Every Married Couple* (Grand Rapids, Mich.: Zondervan Publishing, 1980).

2. Judith Reichman, M.D., *I'm Not in the Mood* (New York, N.Y.: William Morrow & Co., Inc., 1998), 51.

3. Dr. Archibald Hart, *The Sexual Man* (Dallas, Tex.: Word Publishing, 1994).

4. Ibid.

Chapter 9

1. Ruth Myers, *The Perfect Love* (Colorado Springs, Colo.: Waterbrook Press, 1998).

2. Quoted in Elisabeth Elliot, *Gateway to Joy* (Ann Arbor, Mich.: Servant Publications, 1998), 37.

3. John Wimber, "Spirit Song," © 1979 by Maranatha Music, Mercy Publishing.

Chapter 11

1. Quoted in John Piper, *Desiring God* (Portland, Ore.: Multnomah Press, 1986), 127.

Chapter 12

1. R. N. Frost, *Discover the Power of the Bible—How God's Word Can Change Your Life* (Eugene, Ore.: Harvest House Publishers, 2000).

2. Ibid.

3. E. M. Bounds, *A Treasury of Prayer* (Bloomington, Minn.: Bethany House, 1981), 71.

4. Ibid.